Single Mom
the Great yet Rewarding Sacrifice

Speak Life

CHARITY RICKS

Single Mom
THE GREAT, YET REWARDING SACRIFICE

Printed in the United States of America
ISBN: 9798432193230
Copyright © Charity Ricks

Library of Congress Cataloging-in-Publication Data

The copyright laws of the United States of America protect this book. No part of this publication may be reproduced or stored in a retrieval system for commercial gain or profit. Author owns complete rights to this book and may be contracted in regards to distribution.

No part of this publication may be stored electronically or otherwise transmitted in any form or by any means (electronic, photocopy, recording) without written permission of the author.

Scripture quotations are taken from the Holy Bible, New Living Translation (NIV &AMP), copyright © 1996, 2004, 2007, 2013, 2015 by Tyndale House Foundation.
All rights reserved.

Compilation Book Coaching: SynergyEd Consulting/ synergyedconsulting.com
Graphics & Marketing: Greenlight Creations Graphics Designs
glightcreations.com/ glightcreations@gmail.com
Book Cover: MyAsia Reed

shero publishing
sheropublishing.com
getpublished@sheropublishing.com

Single Mom,
THE GREAT, YET REWARDING SACRIFICE

Table of Contents

DEDICATION		6
INTRODUCTION		8
Chapter 1	My Childhood	10
Chapter 2	My Journey as a Single Mom	12
Chapter 3	Overcoming the Shame	16
Chapter 4	Using Welfare as Stepping Stones	22
Chapter 5	Choosing the Right Daycare Provider	26
Chapter 6	The Single Mom and Dating	32
Chapter 7	Yes, I Am a Mom, BUT Who Else Am I?	42
Chapter 8	Single Mom and Self-Care	50
Chapter 9	Single Mom Speaks Life	58
Chapter 10	Single Mom Trusts God to Supply Her Needs	68
Chapter 11	Single Mom and Her Prayer Life	74
Chapter 12	Our Children, Our Blessings, Our Future	82
Chapter 13	Setting Your Child Up in the Right Educational Environment	90
Chapter 14	Single Mom Secures the Bag!	100
Chapter 15	Crushing Your Goals, Working Nine to Five...	106
Chapter 16	Keeping Your Child Engaged in Community Events	114
Chapter 17	Single Mom Networks	122
Chapter 18	He is Faithful to Us!	130
Chapter 19	God Will Restore	136
Chapter 20	The Favor of God	146
Chapter 21	Be Encouraged!	152
ABOUT THE AUTHOR		158

Single Mom
the Great yet Rewarding Sacrifice

Speak Life

Dedication

This book is dedicated to my "support system". My mom, sister, and dad have all played a part, in some way, in helping me to raise my son. Thank You

~Author Charity Ricks

*Her children rise up and call her blessed
(happy, prosperous, to be admired)
Proverbs 31:28 (AMP)*

Introduction:
Single Mom Statistics and Why

The 2020 Census states that there are 9.8 million one-parent households, of which 7.5 million are mother-only households and 2.4 million are father-only households. Let me take a moment to shout out to all the single-parent fathers who are out there working hard making ends meet, doing what's right and raising children by themselves. I Salute you! I want to point out that not all single moms necessarily choose to be a single mom. Some are single moms as a result of unfortunate circumstances such as the death of a spouse, divorce, rape, or an unplanned pregnancy. On the other hand, there are some single moms out there who say being a single mom is a personal choice of theirs'. They say, "I'd rather raise my child by myself"; and they are completely fine with that. Either way, raising a child in a single parent household is a sacrifice and gets tough at times. However, seeing your child walk for the first time, or teaching your child to tie their shoes, write their name, ride a bike, or seeing your child reaching countless other milestones during their childhood is so rewarding.

The very day I began to write this book, just so happened to be National Single Parent Day! I didn't have a clue that we had our own national holiday; however, I truly believe it is well deserved!

CHAPTER 1
My Childhood

I grew up in a two-parent household, meaning both of my parents lived in the house with me. Both of my parents with their incomes put together, I would say were in the lower middle class of working citizens; making just enough to make ends meet. Their highest level of education for both of them was a high school diploma. I remember, that when I was growing up, my mom had to shop for clothes for my younger sister and me at the Goodwill. At that time, my parents were unable to afford named brand clothes and shoes for us. I was in sixth grade when I started noticing that all the other kids wore nice, name brand clothes and nice name brand shoes. They wore the latest fashions during that particular time. It was at that time, I vowed to myself that I did not want to be the adult that was just barely making it, or barely getting by financially. I didn't want my children to have to wear hand-me-downs, nor did I want to have to shop at the Goodwill for my child's clothes.

Don't get me wrong, I'm very grateful for what both of my parents sacrificed to make my childhood as comfortable as possible. However, even as a child, I knew that when I became an adult, financially, I did not want to be scraping the bottom of the barrel. I believe this determination set me up to be a go-getter; I was determined early in life, to go after better... Who knew then that later on down the road, I would be raising a child in a single parent household.

CHAPTER 2
My Journey as a Single Mom

My single parent journey started when I was twenty years old, and is still going strong. I was working a full-time job as a Certified Nursing Assistant, doing private duty work on the side, and enrolled in the local community college, taking prerequisite classes to obtain an Associate Degree. At nineteen, I found out I was pregnant. I stayed busy, but also had a little fun on the side. (If you know what I mean) Yes, I knew Jesus then, but my relationship wasn't tight with Him like it is now. When I found out I was pregnant, my mindset shifted into another gear; I knew I had to buckle down and prepare for the little bundle of joy that was on the way. Having to deal with criticism from others, and being put down and shamed because I became pregnant out of wedlock did not stop me from doing what I knew I had to do. My motto was, "I've come to this speed bump in life; yes, it may slow me down, but I won't let it stop me!" Meaning, I was still going to be a go-getter and go after what I wanted in life; which was a steady job with decent income for me and my child. Also, I was very much aware that I was a single mother, and that I would be raising a young African American male. Too many times, throughout life, our young African

American males become labeled by society. The statistics say that African American males coming from single parent homes are more delinquent. Well, I was determined, and still am, that my son will not be a statistic. I had applied for various assistance programs from Social Services because I knew my goal, my determination and, the vow that I had made with myself when I was younger, to not have my child want for anything. I knew I wanted to be in a better position to provide for and raise my child the right way. I finished summer semester at the community college and had my son soon after. I took a semester out of school to heal and to bond with my son. I applied for the daycare assistance program and other programs to assist me as needed; as stepping stones to what I was in pursuit to accomplish.

As you read through this book, I hope that you find this book to be relatable, educational, encouraging, and inspirational. You will find scriptures and faith-based confessions at the end of each chapter to speak over your life and the life of your children. I pray this book motivates and stirs you up to change negative parental habits into new parental habits that will have positive outcomes. I also pray all my single mothers, guardians and caretakers, out there are blessed by the tips and principles I have used and continue to use in the upbringing of my son. I pray that this book will speak life, and give life, and renew your thinking and propel you to develop a closer relationship with Jesus or to ask Jesus to come into your life and breathe on you and your family and to allow Him to give you a fresh start, and to strengthen, renew, restore, and rejuvenate you as He has entrusted you to take care and be good stewards over the children

He has given you for a season. I pray He gives you the strength and wisdom to raise the children He has entrusted you with, in the admiration of Him. I pray God will use this book as a tool for you to use, to raise up champions and vessels in the earth for His good will, pleasure, and purpose so that He will get all the Glory, Honor and Praise.

Single Mom
NUGGET NOTES

CHAPTER 3
Overcoming the Shame

So, the past few weeks you haven't been yourself, you notice you are sleeping more and your "friend" hasn't shown up for the month, so you decide to take a pregnancy test. The test shows two blue lines or a pink plus sign, depending on which test you used. So just to make sure, you decide to take the second pregnancy test you bought along with the first, just to confirm the accuracy of the first test; and it also shows you are pregnant! Your mind is all over the place and you ask yourself, "What do I do? Do I keep it? Do I give it up for adoption?" The boyfriend already said he doesn't want any children, and gives you an ultimatum to abort the baby or else he will leave. Or your husband whom you thought you knew and loved of many years has decided he no longer wants a family and left you hanging to fend for yourself. You decide to keep the baby and let the chips fall where they may. I applaud you!

While my situation was not quite like this; it was very similar. I too, eventually had to deal with some form of shame. Being raised up in church, hearing the gospel, and my mom raising and instilling values into her girls, one of the things stressed was to wait to have sex until marriage. My parents are the generation of the baby boomers. Therefore, a lot of values and morals like getting married, then having children, creating a family, supporting a household through getting a job or farming (back in their day) were passed down from their parents and into them. So I was brought up with the same values of hard work, going out getting a job and/or a good education and the morals of marriage first, then children. So having to share the news to my immediate family that I was pregnant as an unwed teen, came with shame. I felt shame because I knew I had let my parents down, whatever high standards they had of me, I did not hold up my end of them. Surprisingly, as strict as my dad was, he took it better than what I thought. I thought for sure he was going to kick me out the house. My mind was running and racing, trying to figure where I could stay, because I just knew I was not going to be able to stay at the current address after my dad found out. Even though my dad took it well, I still felt shame; I felt that I had disappointed my loved ones and let them down. I did not know the first thing about raising a baby and I knew I would need help from my mom. The parents of one of my very best friends, shunned her from hanging around me. When I noticed that we were spending less and less time with each other I realized, her parents did not want their daughter to "get any ideas," but to stay focused on going to school to get an education. So we drifted apart. In my church community, I was the only teen pregnant at that time, so of course, that was shameful for me, and I can just imagine how it was for my mom.

So how did I deal with the shame, you may ask? Well, it was my cousin who helped me to see my situation from a different perspective. She said, "Well you aren't the first one to get pregnant out of wedlock, and you sure won't be the last." Being so young, and not knowing what really to do, her statement helped me to see that this happens all the time. That getting pregnant out of wedlock was not uncommon, even though for me it was frowned upon. So, what did I do to help deal with the shame? I repented! I just had some quiet time; just me and the Lord with a Fred Hammond CD playing in the background. I repented. I cried. I told the Lord that I needed help, and that I was sorry for what I had done; I just laid it all out before Him. And that is what God wants us to do with anything. Anytime we mess up; if you have already made Jesus Christ your Lord and Savior and happen to have gotten off track, because we all do, just go to God immediately, pour out your heart before Him and repent (1John 1:9). He will put you back on track. If you have never made Jesus Christ your Lord and Savior, then the verse for you to receive Jesus is Romans 10:9-10 -*If you confess with your mouth the Lord Jesus and believe in your heart that God has raised Jesus from the dead, you shall be saved*. If you would like to receive Jesus, go to the end of this book and pray the prayer to receive Jesus out loud; and when you do, you are automatically in the kingdom of God! Welcome! God knew that your *oops*, or accident would happen before you did. All your mistakes, your *oops moments*, and your *hiccups* were all factored into your life journey, so that *oops* or *surprise* to you, was not an *oops* or *surprise* to God, He knew it would happen before you did. The key is to remember that after you repent, His plan and purpose for your life still remains. God did not change His mind about you!

Let me take a moment and stop here and say that every child was created and destined by our Creator to live. Whatever the situation the baby was conceived, our Creator already knew them. Jeremiah 1:5a of that verse says, *Before I formed you in the womb, I knew you, before you were born, I set you apart.*

Scriptures on Repentance:

For those who have never received Jesus:

If you confess with your mouth the Lord Jesus and believe in your heart that God has raised Jesus from the dead, you shall be saved.
Romans 10:9-10

For those who have received Jesus and have gotten off track and need to repent:

If we confess our sins, he is faithful and just to forgive us our sins and cleanse us from all unrighteousness.
1 John 1:9

For All Who Are In Christ:
There is now no condemnation for those who are in Christ Jesus.
Romans 8:1

Confession to Overcome Shame

Thank you Heavenly Father that because I have confessed my sins to you, I believe you have cleansed me from all unrighteousness and I am free from guilt and shame because your word says that there is now no condemnation for those who are in Christ Jesus. So Heavenly Father I thank you that I act according to the truth of your word, I no longer live a life of guilt and shame.

In Jesus Name,
Amen

CHAPTER 4
Using Welfare as Stepping Stones

Welfare is very beneficial, and there is no shame in having to require a little extra assistance while trying to better yourself. Government assistance programs that can be accessed through social services like WIC, SNAP, daycare vouchers and many others, are there to assist low-income families with obtaining the necessities to properly provide essential care. These programs are especially beneficial for a single mom and her kids. Yes, these programs are awesome to have in your corner, especially when formula for newborns is very expensive and you are already spread thin financially, or you have a desire to go back to school or work, and in need of extra help paying for daycare expenses. However, there comes a time, when as single mothers receiving these benefits, that we should be seeking to raise the bar, and working towards betterment for ourselves and for our family. We should challenge ourselves to come up a little higher; to raise our standard, so to speak.

A wise woman once told me, "It's okay to depend on government assistance for a while, but don't stay there." And that is exactly what I did; I refused to misuse government assistance. Instead, I took advantage of the programs offered through social services, while striving to become a better me. My goal was to get to the point where I was stable on my own without having to use social services. Working for what you want, achieving your goals, and knowing you have God on your side gives you a sense of accomplishment. So, I say utilize all assistance provided to you, such as WIC, daycare vouchers, and food stamps. However, always remember the goal is to use these services as stepping stones until you can do better, if you can. Now, I know people have different circumstances; however, if you are well capable, and know you are well capable of going after better ...why not? I knew I wanted to enroll back in school at the community college. However, I knew I could not afford to pay full price for daycare with a part time salary as a CNA, so I applied for workforce daycare vouchers. When I applied, little did I know that there was a long waiting list for daycare vouchers at the time. So, I signed up; but of course I also believed in a higher power, Jesus, whom I trusted in. I knew that He knew what I needed at the time, in order to achieve what I was trying to do. I used my faith and thanked God for His grace and favor every day, convinced that my name was moving up closer to the top of the list to be a recipient of daycare vouchers. Sure enough, just in time, the lady from social services called me a few days before the start of the spring semester of community college and told me I had been approved for daycare vouchers. Thus I was able to return back to school and work, and put my son in a daycare during the day.

Scriptures:

Therefore I say unto you, whatever you ask for in prayer, believe that you received it, and it will be yours
Mark 11:24 (NIV)

Trust God from the bottom of your heart; don't try to figure out everything on your own. Listen for God's voice in everything you do, everywhere you go; he's the one who will keep you on track.
Proverbs 3:5-6 (MSG)

But my God shall supply all your needs according to His riches and Glory in Christ Jesus
Philippians 4:19 (KJV)

Ask and it will be given to you; seek, and you will find; knock, and it will be opened to you.
Matthew 7:7 (NKJV)

Confession for Trust & Guidance

Dear Gracious Heavenly Father,

I thank you for all that you do. I thank you Father that I can come to you in prayer, and have what I believe that I receive when I pray. Thank you for being my source, and supplying my needs here in the earth. Thank you, Lord, for taking my name from the bottom of the list to the top of the list. As I bring the supplications of my heart to you, I thank you in advance for guiding my steps, opening doors for me no man can shut, and making a way when I may not see a way.

In Jesus Name,
Amen

CHAPTER 5
Choosing the Right Daycare Provider

As a single mom, choosing the right daycare provider is extremely important. I recommend you do a thorough check of any daycare center, take a tour if they will allow it, and speak with all the teachers who will be looking after your child. Search the reviews, seek counsel from others who may have had their child enrolled in the same daycare center or who may know of another parent who may have first-hand knowledge of that center. Always use your gut instinct when something doesn't "sit right" with you when it comes to leaving your child with anyone. I don't care if it's grandma, grandpa, cousin, sister, uncle or a daycare provider. Also do what I call "surprise pop up visits", and just randomly, at odd times of the day when you wouldn't normally show up, pop up at the daycare center. Do a surprise check on your child and make sure they are doing well at the daycare center, because infants can't tell you, "Mommy so and so did this, or Mommy so and so did that." On the other hand, if your child is old enough to talk and they come home telling you something about what a teacher or another child did, and every day you pick your child up and they are telling you the same thing, listen to what your child is saying and check into it, find out what is going on. Don't just assume that your child may or may not know what they are talking about because they are too young to know the difference. Children are smart and pick up on things very quickly. If your child comes home from daycare crying every day and with a complaint about something that happened, and it keeps happening repeatedly, investigate it, check into it, address the matter early on and don't let it get out of hand. Ultimately, your child should feel secure in their environment while out of your presence and care. If you think a certain day care is no longer the right fit for your child, it is absolutely okay to take them out of that daycare and find another one. Because at the end of the day, we want our children to be happy and in healthy environments where they can grow, learn and thrive. Where they thrive, they will always come home with exciting, good news to share.

To this day, my son who is 14 years old remembers a reputable daycare that he was enrolled in possibly from the age of 6-10. He has good memories about that specific daycare, and oftentimes reminisces about the good times he had there in his early childhood. Always make sure the daycare provider is reputable; someone you can trust. I had to place my son in daycare when he was five months old, so I chose a daycare that was associated with my church, around people I knew were the same people that would normally work the nursery during Sunday services. I felt at ease, and at peace with him there. That is another factor, make sure wherever you place your child, you have a peace about where they are, knowing that your child will be well taken care of. If you are in the valley of decisions about a good daycare provider, I recommend speaking with trustworthy friends and relatives who will steer you in the right direction and most importantly pray and ask God to lead you to a good daycare where people are trustworthy and have good character and integrity. You will know what is right if you feel peace on the inside, versus if you feel uneasy. Also, if you have a good support system like family members such as grandma, grandpa, cousin or sister or brother whom you know to be trustworthy and can help you out, that is always, always, always a plus. My support system on the weekend, when daycare was closed was my mom and sister who took "shifts" as they called it, to keep my son for me when I worked "doubles", 16 hour shifts, every Saturday so that I could be in school full time Monday through Friday. Again, locate a good daycare that accepts daycare vouchers, and/or a support system you can **trust** that doesn't mind helping you.

Scriptures:

Where no counsel is, the people fall: but in the multitude of counsellors there is safety.
Proverbs 11:14 (KJV)

If any of you lack wisdom (to guide him through a decision or circumstance), he is to ask of (our benevolent) God, who gives to everyone generously and without rebuke or blame and it will be given him.
James 1:5 (KJV)

Your word is a lamp unto my feet and a light unto my path.
Psalm 119:105 (KJV)

Confession for Guidance

Heavenly Father,

I thank you for who you are. Your word says that if any of you lack wisdom to ask and you will give it to them. Lord, I thank you and ask you to give me wisdom to make decisions in the best interest of my child. I thank you for guiding and ordering my steps to the best daycare provider for my child and any other decisions that I have to make concerning the well-being of my child. Thank you, Lord, for placing people and divine connections in my path to help steer me in the direction I need to go. Thank you that I am obedient to your promptings.

In Jesus Name,
Amen

Single Mom
NUGGET NOTES

CHAPTER 6
The Single Mom and Dating

This topic topic is so important, because sometimes as single women/moms we get lonely. Yes, let's be honest here. We miss having a male companion around, or a male companion to talk to. So, we step out, and start dating and there is nothing wrong with that. But you don't want to be so desperate to have a man that you just fall for anything that has "breath and britches". I saw a Facebook meme the other day that had lyrics from the song, *After the Rain,* by Betty Wright (God bless her soul) - *Havin' a piece of a man is better than havin' no man at all. So I'ma just take what I got and work with it.* Nah, Aunt Betty! That is not what we are going after these days! Hello, somebody?? As a single mom, we must remember that we are not only dating for ourselves, but for our kids as well. I may have gotten a few side-eyes on this one. But truth be told, we are a package deal, Right?! Okay, so yeah, he may be helping you with the bills, but your kids don't get along with him or are uneasy around him, causing disruption in the home and disturbing peace in the home?! Single moms, it is so important that we don't just bring any and every man around our children; especially if we don't know them that well. In this day and time, a background check would not be a bad idea, just to make sure the guy who you are talking to isn't a registered sex offender, or stalker, or worse. I hate to sound extreme, or to put fear in anyone, but these days we are living in, are a whole lot worse than the days when our parents were kids. The bible says, in the last days the hearts of many will wax cold and people will be lovers of themselves. So take extra measures to make sure you and your children are around someone safe. I believe it should be a new normal for all single women to adopt. I love watching Tyler Perry movies, and my favorite is- *I Can Do Bad All by Myself,* starring Taraji P Henson, my favorite female actress. The movie is about three kids who had to move in with their aunt (Taraji) and her boyfriend because their caretaker, who was their grandmother, had passed away. Later in the movie you start to see how their aunt's boyfriend began to look at the oldest girl in a sexual way and began to harass her. One night the oldest girl was in the kitchen to get her brother's insulin and her aunt's boyfriend came into the kitchen with her and picked her up and put her on top of the counter and tried to rape her. When the aunt came into the kitchen, her boyfriend lied and said the girl tried to seduce him. Her niece was crying and saying- "No, no it was him; he was trying to rape me!" At first it appears as though the aunt had taken the boyfriend's side as she told him to go upstairs and she would draw him a bath. However, she saw right through her boyfriend's lies, because unfortunately when she was a child, her mom's boyfriend raped her. When she told her mom, her mom didn't believe her, which was devastating. So many children fall victim to abuse from "live in boyfriends" of single mothers who just want a man around, just to say they have one. When in actuality, the boyfriend is harming the child(ren), and in some cases the mother is too blind to see and won't even protect their child(ren). Instead the mother will "assist" the boyfriend in abusing their child. Sometimes the mom is too afraid of the boyfriend to put an end to the abuse. Please note that abuse can come in many forms. Abuse can be physical, verbal, mental, or emotional. The boyfriend can intimidate through controlling behaviors such as imposed isolation (where he doesn't want you to see friends of family members), narcissism and manipulation. All abuse is unhealthy and toxic and you and your children should be free from that. So please, my single moms ,here are a few tips to go by when dating:

Tip#1: If you are starting a friendship with a male (not dating yet) take some time and see how it goes between you and him. Pay attention to conversations; you learn a lot about a person by what and how they communicate. A lot of us use our intuition and can pick up on things quickly. If you hear something that doesn't sit right with you, ask more questions. Don't let him come over to your house yet, because if y'all don't click, then it probably won't go any further. At least, he won't know where you stay, and he wouldn't have met the kids. No heartache and no trouble.

Tip#2: If you and your "friend" have been talking for quite some time, and you are actually (dating), then have him come over and meet the kids. Ladies, I know some of us are guilty of doing this, but when it comes time to introduce your friend to your kids, introduce your friend as Mr. So and So, **not** *Uncle* So and So. I know some of you may be laughing right now, because you know it is the truth.

Only thing wrong with that is, whenever Uncle So and So comes around, you and him are tongue kissing and touchy-feely, and the kids see all of that and become confused. Based upon what they see, they think it's "okay" for your friend to do those things under the title of "Uncle." Think about it. This can be a problem, and lead to other things, because if a real uncle in the family who is inappropriately touchy-feely with your child, the child may think it's okay. Therefore, they may not tell that they have been touched inappropriately by the uncle because that is what they have observed in the home. I assume we are all responsible adults, but just in case some were wondering, we should always break it down to our kids at their level; a level in which they can clearly understand what is right and what is wrong. Explain that if they have been touched inappropriately by *anyone,* they should immediately tell an adult who they trust. Don't just ask your children one time about sexual contact; ask periodically to remind them that inappropriate talk, touching or anything that makes them uncomfortable whether by another child or an adult is wrong. Let your children know that they can come to a safe haven to tell about the abuse without feeling embarrassed, or without feeling like they did something wrong.

Tip#3: Observe your friend's behavior and how he interacts with your kids on a regular basis, *in your presence*. Don't ever leave your children in the hands of your boyfriend too early; without fully knowing how he responds and acts around your kids. If you notice he is slighting any of your children(acting or treating your kids differently in a negative way) from how he treats you, he's probably not the one, Sis. Don't go any further with this man, because your child(ren) should feel just as safe, accepted and loved around your friend as you do. Listen to how he talks to your kids. If you hear any talk that is belittling or damaging your child's self-esteem, if he is cursing at your child or constant picking with your child, or talking to your child in a tone in which you would not talk to your child in, he is probably not the one. If he always wants to do things with you, but never wants to do activities to include your child, that is another red flag, Sis. Please heed these warning signs that he is probably not the one. If he flat out tells you that he doesn't think he can date a woman who has kids (this has been said to me before) then just drop it, don't try to make it work because it won't. You can't change that person's opinion about the matter. I once heard a wise man say, "a man forced against his will, is of the same opinion still"; meaning you may can persuade a man into being in a relationship with you, but is his heart with you? He may only be tolerating you for the sex, and his heart not be with you. That's the difference. I can tell you from experience, in the end it does not work. Why? Let me say it again. Because "a man forced against his will, is of the same opinion still." And having a man around just to say, "I have a man", but his heart is not with you or your children, what good is that, Sis? If your child comes to you and confides in you that they are uncomfortable around your friend, or they don't feel safe around your friend, take that into consideration. You must heed these warnings when they come from a child of any age. However, my personal opinion is that younger children, especially can pick up on and tell you when something isn't right with a person. A young child may express their feelings in their own unique way. So watch and listen; pay close attention to what your children are saying.

Tip #4: Limit different men (specifically who you may call boyfriend) from coming in and out of your house, as this isn't a good look, and our children are sponges, they soak in e-v-e-r-y-t-h-i-n-g. They say and copy everything we say and do thinking it's okay. Also, for my boy moms (I'm one), we have another reason to be careful, because our sons do tend to be a little more defensive and take on a protective mentality over us, as their moms. So if your friend is over, and your friend says or does something to you that your son doesn't like, he just may come to your defense. Don't be shocked and don't scold him. Just know it's because your son loves you and knows you're being disrespected. For my girl moms, as a woman we should want to make sure that we are not setting the example in front of them that they will mimic that will later on make them acquire a name for themselves that they don't want to stick with them such as being "easy".

Tip #5: If he curses you or tries to raise a hand at you when he gets mad, he is not the one! Move on! Let him go immediately! More than likely, if he disrespects you, he will disrespect and mistreat your child(ren). A wise man once said, "Go by the *one-time rule*." Meaning, he's got one time to curse you, and one time to raise his hand at you! If this happens, chunk up your deuces and see him out the door ASAP! Don't make excuses for him if he did curse you or raise his hand at you as if he was going to hit you. Nope, that's it! It's a wrap!

Because if he did it once and got away with it; more than likely, he will do it again. And you can't complain about what you tolerate.

I know it may seem like a lot, and really there is a lot more that we can go more in depth in, but maybe we will delve deeper in another book. Every woman has what's called a woman's intuition, you know when you have a gut feeling that something just isn't quite right, or you feel led to do something. We must make sure we listen to our woman's intuition; and most importantly, pray and ask God for wisdom and discernment when it comes to choosing the right man we allow to come into our lives and be a part of "our" world as single moms. Let's remember, ladies- we are the prize, and we are also a *package deal*!

Scriptures:

The {reverent} fear of the Lord is the beginning of wisdom; all those who practice it have a good understanding.
Psalm111:10 (ESV)

For the word of God is living and powerful, and sharper than any two-edged sword, piercing even to the division of soul and spirit, and of joints and marrow, and is a discerner of the thoughts and intents of the heart.
Hebrews 4:12 (NKJV)

Discretion will watch over you; Understanding and discernment will guard you.
Proverbs 2:11 (AMP)

A wise man will hear, and increase learning, and a man of understanding will attain wise counsel.
Proverbs 1:5 (NKJV)

Confession for Wisdom and Discernment

Dear God,

I thank you for giving me sound judgement and discernment and the wisdom to be able to differentiate between those whom you have sent versus the ones sent by the enemy. Thank you Lord that my spiritual ears are in tune to hear you speaking, and that I am on high alert to when something or someone has come with bad intentions. Remove any and all blindfolds the enemy tries to use to prevent me from seeing the truth. Thank you, Lord, for revealing truth and help me to operate on a higher level of discernment and wisdom when dating. I ask that you remove any one from my life that has not been sent from you, and bring the right person into my life whom you have for me. Thank you, God, for giving me the strength to not look back or go back to the things you have delivered me out of that do not conform to your will, plan, or purpose for my life and my child(ren's) life.

In Jesus Name
Amen

Single Mom
NUGGET NOTES

CHAPTER 7
Yes, I Am a Mom, BUT Who Else Am I? Knowing Who I am in Christ!

Being a single mom, we often times find ourselves, placing ourselves on the back burner as we become consumed and engulfed into our children's day-to-day activities; from school tutoring, to after school sports, to being a taxi cab driver, chauffeuring your kids and their friends to and from various places. You may be known as a soccer mom who brings snacks and drinks for your child's entire soccer team after every practice and after every game And yes, that is a joy. However, I am here to tell you, that you are not just a soccer mom, you are not just the mom who is a chauffeur for your children's team mates! In *any* relationship, it is so easy to become wrapped up or engulfed in the relationship that we tend to lose ourselves and who we are. I want you to know that we are fearfully and wonderfully made. God took the time to design us according to His likeness. As God once told me, *every little intricate detail I created on your body, it was meant to be there*. Same is true for you. From the little black, flat mole on your face, to the beautiful freckles. Yes, God took the time to make each of us special, unique and different. There isn't another human being on this earth who has the exact same fingerprints or marks that you have. You are an individual; unique, set apart, and chosen. You are beautiful. In the book of

Genesis, first chapter, it said that God created the heaven and the earth, day, night, the ocean and waters, dry land, grass yielding herb. After each of these things He made, He looked at it and said, "It is Good". Don't you know that after God formed you and created you and wove you in your mother's womb with love in every intricate detail, he looked at you and said, 'It is Good". How then do we have the audacity to look at ourselves in the mirror and say, "If I only didn't have freckles on my face, I would be beautiful. If only my skin was a little darker or lighter, or if only I had high cheek bones, or if my lips were thinner, or fuller, then I would be beautiful." When the truth is, when your Creator created you, He looked at you and said, "It is Good". How awesome is that! How then, can we call something bad to the very thing God created and looked at and said, "It is Good"? Then He placed seeds of greatness on the inside of each one of us so that as we grow in Him. His desires become our desires, and we end up walking and moving into our God-given purpose for our lives as we follow and are led by God. As we are led by God, we are used by Him and become a vessel for Him in the earth. The bible says that- *when you were in your mother's womb, I knew you.* You are valuable and important; God has placed gifts and talents inside of you that will help someone else. When God blessed you with gifts and talents, He wasn't just thinking about you alone, he also had others in mind.

We all know this thing called *life* comes with trials and tribulations; sometimes back to back. You may be like, "What is really going on? I can't handle this. This is too much!" Sometimes the very things we go through, could be the very things to help someone else go through similar situations. Sometimes God uses us as forerunners to help pave the way for someone else that we may not even know. God works with not just you and me in mind, but with others in mind as well. Sometimes the things that happen to us that we find to be a hard blow or hit and the God-given strategies we use to navigate and maneuver through life's mess, can help the next person coming behind us. The *mess* life throws at you can become your *message* to someone else of how you overcame and conquered. Your *message* can help the next person coming behind you, so they can know that with God they can overcome and conquer, too! Sometimes life trials and tribulations can leave you depleted; feeling overwhelmed, hopeless, and discouraged. You feel like you are unworthy, undervalued, and underappreciated. Know that you are valuable, worthy and appreciated! Know that your worth comes from the blood Jesus shed on the cross for you. Being reminded that He purchased you with His blood helps to keep things in perspective; knowing who you are, your value and your worth. You are a crowned jewel, a royal diadem in the eyes of God. A lot of times we base our value and worth on what society tells us our value and worth should be. Society tells us you are valuable or worthy if you wear designer clothing. Society tells us that the more money we make, the more valuable we are. But I heard a wise man say that, "your self-worth is not determined by your net worth." Money is not what makes you valuable. If you had one-million dollars or one dollar in the bank, you still carry the same worth and value because of who you are and whose you are. Good God almighty, Wheew! Did you catch that? If this isn't blessing you, it is definitely blessing me as I'm writing this! Again, our worth and value is solely wrapped up in the blood of Jesus that was shed for us on Calvary. As women, we all have done things, we are not completely proud of. Some things you may say, will only be between you and Jesus, and that is fine. Know that God does not condemn us, but convicts us to repentance and reproves and chastens us because He loves us. If He did not love us, he would not reprove, or chasten us. Just like you would correct your child when your child gets out of line, so it is as a child of God. We also get corrected because God wants us to grow in Him so that He can take us higher in Him. You may say, "Well, I have five children, and they all have different daddies, been through a divorce, gone through domestic violence, been raped, had several abortions, I'm not worthy to be loved, I have no value." It's easy to feel like you are unworthy and undervalued; some women my even think they are damaged goods. But remember as a woman, you are worthy and valuable, you are God's precious jewel, God's prized possession, the apple of God's eye, you are His masterpiece, His workmanship, you are a daughter of the King, you are blood-bought, purchased by the precious blood of Jesus who died for you and me, you are royalty and in the royal family of God! If you haven't received Jesus in your life and would like to be in the Royal family of God, you can pray the prayer of salvation at the end of this book and receive Jesus in your life, and begin to speak over your life the same things that God says you are.

I love to listen to Joyce Meyer. She has a powerful testimony of how she overcame being sexually abused by her biological dad and how she overcame the struggles of not feeling worthy and thinking she would never experience the best in life because of what happened to her. In other words, she thought she was damaged goods. But she was able to turn her thinking around by reading her bible, praying and allowing God to renew her mind in many areas of her life. Eventually, she began seeing herself the way God saw her. Sometimes, how we see ourselves is totally different from how God sees us. It's so easy to only look at who or what we are through our lens/eyes and not consider looking at ourselves through God's lens of His eyes. In God's eyes we are righteousness of God (meaning we are in right standing with him), we are without spot or blemish, we are blameless in His sight. Wow, if we can learn this, myself included, to always remember to look at ourselves through the eyes of God, it will boost our self-confidence and self-esteem and how we see ourselves. We will act accordingly to who we are and that is a child of the Highest! A daughter of the King! Royalty!

We are His trophy. You are not damaged goods, Sis. Don't think that just because you have children that there isn't a man in the world that would want you. I know that is what the world says, I believe that God has a husband for me, and a husband for you (if that's your desire) The husband that God has for us, will already be equipped to handle the responsibility and have what it takes to help raise someone else's children as his own and lead by a Godly example in the home. So no, don't feel like you've missed out on the best things in life because of your past mistakes. God has a way of restoring what the canker worm and locusts have eaten. In other words, God will give back more than what was lost or stolen from you. We will leave that up to Him, and how He wants to do it. Nothing is too far gone that God can't restore or give back to us greater than what we lost. It could be our peace, joy, and happiness. Someone may have lost their childhood by having to act as the parent to their younger siblings. I believe that God can make it up to you even in your adult years. God sees all, and He knows all. He wants the very best for His children. He is good and the source of all good things. He says in His word that no good thing will he withheld from you. So, know that you are valuable and worthy to be loved the right way. God says, He watches over the sparrows, so of course he will look out for you and me; aren't you worth much more than they?!

Scriptures:

But now the Lord who created you, O Israel, says: Don't be afraid, for I have ransomed you; I have called you by name you are mine.
Isaiah 43:1 (NLT)

You are precious to me, and I have given you a special place of honor. I love you. That is why I am willing to trade others, to give up whole nations, to save your life.
Isaiah 43:4 (ERV)

But [you were actually purchased] with precious blood, like that of a [sacrificial] lamb unblemished and spotless, the priceless blood of Christ.
1Peter 1:19 (NLT)

He chose to give birth to us by giving us his true word. And we, out of all creation, became His prized possession
James 1:18 (NLT)

The LORD has declared today that you are his people, his own special treasure, just as he promised, and that you must obey all his commands.
Deuteronomy 26:18 (NLT)

Confession For Seeing Myself The Way HE Sees Me

Heavenly Father,

Your word declares that I am blood bought and I am precious in your sight. Therefore, I declare that I am worthy and valued because of your blood shed for me on the cross, thank you father that I am your child, therefore, I am your special treasure, prized possession, and I am the apple of your eye, have royalty flowing in my veins; therefore, I am royalty and belong to the royal family of God. I thank you that I operate in the confidence, boldness, and power that you have given me, help me to see myself the way you see. Lord I thank you that on days when I feel unworthy, help me to be remember who I am in you. I am yours and I am made in your image, of your likeness and I will carry myself as such.

In Jesus Name,
Amen.

CHAPTER 8
Single Mom and Self-Care

As a single mom, at the end of a busy day of work in the office, you then come home and play with the kids, clean up the house a little to try to make it look decent, cook dinner, help with homework, get the kids bathed and ready for the next day. Much is required of you. Therefore, it is vitally important that you find the time to care for yourself daily. As it is very easy to become overwhelmed, stressed, tired and burnt out just from day-to-day activities. Self-care is defined as *taking an active role in protecting one's own well-being and happiness, in particular during periods of stress*. The saying is that "you can't pour from an empty glass"; so that means filling yourself up, restoring, and reviving yourself so that you can effectively do what it is you need to do to take care of others. I also learned the importance of self-care from my mom.

I started out as a fairly young mother; my mom told me that it was okay to go out and still have fun. I was twenty years old when my son was born. I remember when I did go back out for the first time to socialize and just have some *me* time. I believe I attended a house party. I didn't feel right; I felt like I was supposed to be at home looking after my son. I was feeling a sense of guilt for being out and having fun. Ladies, let me tell you, never ever feel guilty about taking time for yourself to have fun, hang with your girlfriends and take a trip out of town. It is okay! Especially if you work hard during the week going to work, and to school and still providing food, clothes, shelter, and overall stability for your kids. You make sure you are doing right by your kids. Yes! You deserve some mommy time!

Self-care looks different to different women and is manifested in a lot of different ways based upon what each woman likes. For instances, for one person's self-care can be soaking in the tub with her favorite bath salts or bath bombs(that's personally one of my favs); for others, it can be reading a book, praying, meditating, or having a soothing cup of hot tea or coffee before bed. Others can experience self-care by reading a scripture or passage from the bible, listening to relaxing jazz music, going to comedy shows, hanging with your girlfriends, or taking a trip without the kids. Self-care can even be laying down on your bed or couch in a peaceful environment and resting, indulging in one of your favorite candle fragrances, enjoying a little retail therapy or just doing absolutely nothing at all (another one of my favorites). It's always good to get in touch with your feminine side; especially if you are a mom who wears yoga pants and ponytails all day or you seem to constantly be in uniform scrubs attire all day (that's me). Get in touch with your feminine side by dressing up; putting on your heels or wedges, a cute dress, or jeans dressed up to make it more than just a casual look. Put on your face (makeup), accessorize with jewelry or a cute pocketbook or wristlet and matching shoes. Get a fresh hairdo. Just getting dolled up can make you feel so good about yourself; how you look and feel can boost your self-image, confidence, and just make you feel beautiful overall. I saw a meme once that said, *no matter how you feel, get up, get dressed (dolled up), show up and show out!* It's okay! Take time for yourself and do not feel guilty about it, and don't let anyone else make you feel guilty for taking some mommy time. It is needed, you deserve it, and most importantly, your kids deserve the best version of their mommy they can get. You can't be the best version of you as a mother when you are broke down, tired, busted and disgusted! So, what are you waiting for? Get that self-care routine started today!

Scriptures for Self-Care: MIND, BODY, and SPIRIT

MIND:

Therefore do not be anxious about tomorrow, for tomorrow will be anxious for itself. Sufficient for the day is its own trouble.
Matthew 6:34 (NLT)

For God has not given us a spirit of fear, but of power and of love and of a sound mind.
2 Timothy1:7 (NKJV)

BODY:

Do you not know that your bodies are temples of the holy spirit, who is in you, whom you have received from God? You are not your own; you were bought at a price. Therefore, Honor God with your bodies.
1Corinthians 6:19-20 (NIV)

So whether you eat or drink, do it all for the glory of God.
1 Corinthians 10:31 (NIV)

SPIRIT:

But grow in the grace and knowledge of our Lord and Savior Jesus Christ. To him be the glory both now and to the day of eternity. Amen.
2 Peter 3:18 (ESV)

But the fruit of the spirit is Love, joy, peace, patience, kindness, goodness, faithfulness, gentleness, self-control, against such things there is no law.
Galatians 5:22 (ESV)

Confession for Self-Care of the Body

Heavenly Father,

I thank you that I am learning what it means to allow myself to engage in self-care. I believe your will is for me to take care of this temple you dwell in as a form of self-care. So God I thank you that my body is operating the way you designed it, without use of medications to regulate my body. My body as God's temple, I am His mobile home, therefore I am particular to what I eat and drink, I choose to eat foods that will properly nourish my body to fuel my body of the proper nutrients it needs to be able to do the work God has called me to, here in the earth. I chose foods that are as close to the way God originally intended for them to be, which includes fresh fruits and fresh plant-based foods. I speak life over my body in Jesus Name, My body is free from sickness and disease. I allow my body the proper rest it needs to function from day to day. I declare that I have good sleep every night. My sleep is sweet so that my body can properly repair itself; every cell, every muscle tissue is repaired and my body is re-energized as I sleep to allow me to wake refreshed, rejuvenated and re-energized to continue to perform God's work here on the earth. I exercise my body to keep myself tone and fit physically for the Master's use.

In Jesus Name,
Amen!

Confession for Self-Care of the Mind

Heavenly Father,

I thank you that you created my mind and my intellect. I thank you that I come up higher in my thinking Lord to please you. I thank you that you have not given me the spirit of fear, but of power of love and of a sound mind. So, Lord I thank you that I have a sound mind. Father, I thank you that I have supernatural recall, therefore my memory is blessed. Thank you, Lord, that I think thoughts that are pure, lovely and of good report. My thoughts are pleasing in your sight. I choose to set my mind on things above and keep it set. My mind is renewed as I spend time in your Word. I cast down imaginations, and every high thing that exalts itself against the knowledge of God, bringing every thought into captivity to the obedience of Christ. I plead the blood of Jesus over my mind and every attack of the enemy on my mind is defeated and cancelled in Jesus Name. I rebuke the spirit of anxiety, worry and depression because they are unlawful in heaven, therefore it is unlawful in the earth. So, I bind up anxiety, depression and all diseases that do not line up with the word of God and loose for ministering spirits to bring about calmness and peace and stability of mind in Jesus Name. I protect my peace of mind by only allowing positive vibes and thoughts, anyone or anything that disturbs my peace of mind I remove myself from it. I protect and value my peace of mind in Jesus Name. Your word says "be not anxious for nothing but by prayer and supplication make your needs and wants known to God." So, I come to you God with this prayer over my mind that you bless it, preserve it, and cover it in your blood.

In Jesus Name,
Amen.

Confession for Self-Care of the Spirit

Lord,

I thank you that you created me as a tri-partied being. I am a Spirit, I have a soul and I live in a physical body. Lord I speak to my Spirit. I thank you that my Spirit (inner man) is continually built up in Christ. My inner man is strong as I spend time in the Word of God so that I can stand securely on the word of God when trouble comes. I am careful of what I watch and listen to because I don't want to grieve the Holy Spirit. Therefore, I limit myself from watching or listening to anything that grieves the Holy Spirit. I listen and watch things that increase my faith and strengthen my inner man. My spirit man is strong, I speak in my heavenly language daily to strengthen my inner man, I speak in my heavenly language as a weapon against spiritual warfare for the word says, 'for we do not fight against flesh and blood but principalities and rulers of darkness', therefore I put on the whole armor of God, using the sword of the spirit which is the word of God to stand against the enemy. I thank you for giving me the grace to operate in the Character of the Holy Spirit which includes Love, Joy, Peace, Long suffering, Patience, Kindness, Goodness, Faithfulness, Gentleness, and Self-control. I'm being renewed day-by-day in your Word so that my life can exemplify Christ-likeness so that I can be a witness to the lost in the earth.

In Jesus Name,
Amen.

Single Mom
NUGGET NOTES

CHAPTER 9
Single Mom Speaks Life

As a born-again Christian, the most important aspect in a believer's life is to walk by faith! Everything we, the believers, desire in life should line up with the word of God through our faith. If you don't get anything else out of this book, please pay attention to this chapter. For me, my faith was how I was able to manifest into my life what I desired pertaining to my son and myself from his infant days and my early twenties, even until this present day. Simply put, faith is believing God and thanking Him for what He has already done for you, that you don't yet see manifested; faith is using your words(confessions)as go-getters. The bible teaches that life and death is in the power of the tongue; you have what you *say* on a consistent basis. Confessing is to simply say out loud and bring our words in agreement with what God's word (the bible) says about our situation/circumstance. So, if you want to see good things come your way, *speak life*. No, for those who are unfamiliar with how faith works, this does not have anything to do with witchcraft. Jesus also used his words to create the heavens and the earth. In Genesis, Chapter 1(TLB), it says, *the earth was a shapeless, chaotic mass. God <u>said,</u> "Let there be light." And God was pleased with it. And God <u>said,</u> "Let the vapors separate to form the sky above and the oceans below"*. God saw what he <u>said</u>. Then it says, *God <u>said,</u> "Let the earth burst forth with every sort of grass and seed bearing plant, and fruit trees with seeds inside the fruit." And God was pleased.* God <u>saw</u> what He <u>said</u> (declared). If you are tired of your life being in a chaotic mess, start using your words to create what you want to see happen in your life that is in agreement to what God wants for your life. And God lets us know in Jeremiah 29:11, which says, *"For I know the thoughts and plans that I have for you", says the Lord, "thoughts and plans for welfare and peace and not for evil, to give you hope in your final outcome";* that no good thing will He withhold from you. So, when I learned this in my early twenties, when my son was still an infant, I wrote out a list of confessions based on what the word of God said about my circumstances at that given time.

Getting into your bible and reading it, you will find out more of what God's will is for you, and how He wants you, as His child, to succeed and prosper. I know some people find it hard to read and understand the bible, especially using the King James version. However, there are other versions available that will breakdown down all the *Thus* and *Thees* and *Thous* to modern day terms to allow you to read and understand clearly. One of my favorite translations, is "The Message" translation; it really breaks down the verses without taking away from or watering down the scriptures; giving simplicity and making it enjoyable to read. I mentioned earlier that I had my name placed on a waiting list to receive daycare vouchers because I could not afford to pay full price for the cost of childcare. I distinctly remember the lady telling me that there was a long waiting list, and that it would probably be six months or more before my name would get to the top of the list. What I was striving for was to have my son in daycare in six months so that I could return to school. I went home. I knew the word God said, *"I will supply all your needs according to my riches and glory in Christ Jesus."* I wrote down my declaration of faith (confession) and began to confess/speak it out loud daily. I said it until I saw it. So, it went something like this: God, I thank you for favor, that my name will rise to the top of the list for daycare vouchers in less than six months, thank you God for providing my needs in Jesus Name. I also had other words of declaration of faith that I spoke over my son, some went like this: Thank you Lord that I am raising my son in the admiration of you, that my son will grow up and serve you. Thank you, Lord, for giving me grace to be the mom you have called me to be in Jesus Name. Thank you, Lord, that my son will have wisdom beyond his years In Jesus Name. I had a list of faith declarations written out and taped it on the wall next to my son's changing table, so that every time I changed him, I would be reminded to speak my declarations of faith.

A. ***Speaking life* over your children is very important.** Lately, I've been seeing posts on Facebook of parents referring to their children as their "broke best friend." So, you're saying that your child is your best friend, and your best friend is broke? Already? The child is only five years old. Can we let our children be great first, before calling them broke? How about saying "my best friend the billionaire"? *Speak life* over your children; speak over them what you want to see in their life. If you always catch little Johnny in a lie when questioning him, instead of saying, "Johnny, you're a liar", how about saying the opposite? When you speak over little Johnny, say, " Johnny you are a young man of integrity, and you always speak truth." Another example is, if your child is failing in his classes, don't call him a failure and say that he will never be anything in life. Instead say, "You can do all things through Christ who strengthens you; you excel academically and everything you put your hands to do is blessed and succeeds." A tip I would give to all moms is, start *speaking life* over your children at a young age, teaching them this practice at a young age so that they can have a head start in using it in life. You know the saying- *when we know better, we ought to do better.*

I'm reminded of the movie, *War Room;* if you haven't seen it yet, I recommend you check it out. There is one scene where the mom, played by Priscilla Shirer, has a list of her prayer confessions for what she was believing God for in her situation, taped to the wall inside of her prayer closet. Later in the movie, it shows how her daughter, who was maybe eight or nine years old, had her confessions taped on her wall based on what she was believing God for. Faith confessions is a valuable concept to teach your children early in life that will be with them from childhood through adulthood. It teaches them at an early age that we can use our faith to access *our stuff* that God has put our name on in the spiritual realm to claim it in the natural realm. I remember when my son was younger, I would have him repeat after me, confessions to start his day. The key is to start with children while they are young and be consistent to stick with it. Sometimes, once they become teenagers, they think they know it all. Waiting until then to teach this concept and getting them to apply it to their lives may be an uphill battle. It's easy to slack off your confessions; don't beat yourself up about it, just get back on track and stick with it until you see the manifestation of what you've been speaking! Hold fast the confession of your faith!

B.   We can also start and set our days based on the words we speak. We can speak to our day and declare what we want from our day. Here are some of the declarations I say: "This is the day the Lord has made. I will rejoice and be glad in it". God wants us to continually be in expectation. My pastor says, "expectation is the breeding ground for miracles", so I also say, "I expect something good to happen to me today. I am a blessing; I expect a blessing and I will experience blessings on this day. I speak protection over my family and loved ones and declare, God, that you are keeping me and my family from hurt, harm and danger. I plead the blood of Jesus over my child, my day and my family. I pray over my family that we will go to and from our destinations safely." You can bind up the enemy with your words and declare what to see happen in your day. You can pray and ask God for a smooth day. I often say it like this, "Lord thank you for going before me this day, making my crooked path straight and removing anything from my path meant to destroy me or cause me to stumble."

Now, this is not to say that nothing will ever happen in your day that you don't like, because the bible says that there is an enemy loose seeking whom he may devour. Also, we deal with different types of people on the job, in the school and everywhere that is "public space". We are around both saved and unsaved people, and some who are witches and warlocks who are workers of witchcraft. However, we have a covenant with God Almighty and he promises us in Isaiah 54:17 that - *No weapon formed against you shall prosper, this is the inheritance from the Lord.* So, the weapons may form, but they will not prosper. Hallelujah!! We must remember in Romans 8:28, *that all things work together for the good of those who love the Lord.* Also, we must remember Psalm 34:19 that declares, *many are the afflictions of the righteous but the lord delivers him out of them all.* There have been so many times when Satan uses people to try to come against me. Some may be wondering why I say that it is Satan and not the person who comes up against me. Here's why; we must remember that as a child of God, we wrestle not against flesh and blood, but against principalities, and rulers of darkness. It is Satan who is using the person to attack us and the person whom he uses isn't even aware he is being used by Satan. We must not be mad at the person but to call out the evil spirit that is working in the person. Say, "Devil, I see what you are trying to do, and I rebuke you in Jesus Name! You are under my feet! I have authority over you!" Now, don't go calling people the devil and saying, " Get thee behind me, Satan" to their face. Remember, it is not the person, but demonic, spiritual forces using the person. Walk away and go to the bathroom or somewhere off to yourself and begin to pray (I've done this before);bind and rebuke the enemy. In Matthew: Chapter 16, when Peter made a comment to Jesus before Jesus was to go to be crucified saying- "No, impossible!" (paraphrasing). Jesus knew that it was Satan that was speaking through Peter, and not Peter himself. Jesus said, "Get thee behind me, Satan." Notice, Jesus didn't say, "Get thee behind me, Peter." No, Jesus said, "Get thee behind me, Satan." Jesus knew that Satan was using Peter to talk him out of the things of God. Remember, that in Christ we have the Victory!

C.   ***Speaking life*** **over our finances is also important.** Just like we speak life over other aspects in our lives, we should also speak life over our bank accounts and our monies. God wants His people to prosper. As a tither (giving 10% of all your income and increase to God) and a giver of offerings, which is given to your local church where you are being taught the Word of God, you are granted a covenant right between you and God. As a result of the covenant right, you can claim protection from the devourer(satan) (Malachi 3:11). You can expect God to supernaturally bless the rest of your monies and to meet you at your need. Back when I was working my part time job, I made sure to honor God with my tithes and offerings, because I knew that it was because of Him that I was able to do all that I was doing and that He was making a way for me. I also knew that I could not have done any of the things I was doing without Him on my side, in my corner, and having my back! When God's got your back, you already know you will be well taken care of. As the scriptures say, *I have never seen the righteous forsaken, nor His seed begging bread. (*Psalm 37:25). In other words, God takes care of His children! As I speak life over my finances, I say, "My finances are blessed. God is opening the windows of heaven for me and pouring out a blessing that I will not have room enough to receive. My money is blessed, all my bank accounts are blessed, I have miracle money and miracle increase in my house. Wealth and riches are in my house, my storehouses; my bank accounts are filled with plenty. God will supply all my needs according to His riches and His glory in Christ Jesus. I am abundantly supplied; all my needs are met". *The Lord is my Shepherd (to feed, guide and protect me), I shall not want(lack).(*Psalm 23: 1)

D.   ***Speaking life*** **over your body, mind, health.** Regular exercise, drinking water, eating healthy, keeping vision and dental appointments and getting annual physicals are all essential to maintaining a healthy body and mind.. We must not neglect our body when it is telling us something is wrong. When we look good and feel good, especially in our clothes, then it boosts our self-image. I myself, am learning that staying healthy is just as important to God as any other aspect in our life. It is important to stay healthy for God. When we are healthy, we are zealous, vibrant, energetic and able to do and be all that God has called us to do and be. Feeling sluggish and tired will impede how much you can get done. *Speaking life* and health to our bodies, in the bible, John prays- *Beloved, I pray above all things that thou mayest prosper and be in health even as your soul prospers* (3John 2). Speaking to our minds we say, "God has not given us the spirit of fear, but of power and of love and of a sound mind. My mind is blessed, I am healthy in my body, my body functions the way God designed it to function, and I rebuke the enemy from trying to attack my body." If you are experiencing some ailments in your body, speak to those ailments and then say what God says about it. "You are healed!" Jesus took 39 stripes for us. It is said that there are 39 classifications of diseases in the world today, so with that being said, Jesus took a stripe for every disease known to mankind and bore it for us on the cross so that we would not have to bear it. 1 Peter 2:25 -the last part of that verse says, *by His stripes, we are healed.* When we look at the word disease, we can break it down into *dis-ease*. Jesus does not want us to be at *dis-ease* about anything. I'm learning this myself, as I'm learning to trust Him at greater levels. We must continue to grow in God and come up higher in Him. He wants us not to worry, and not to be stressed out; 1Peter 5:7 (NIV) tells us to *cast all your anxiety on him because he cares for you.* If we are constantly at *dis-ease* and holding tight to cares and worries, what does that do to our bodies? What will a lot of stress do to our bodies? For one, it will break our bodies down, and cause our bodies not to function like they should. Diseases can begin to enter our bodies. For example, diseases or conditions such as hypertension which can lead to other medical issues such as stroke, or diabetes from poor eating habits and lack of exercise, or dehydration and constipation from lack of water intake, or insomnia and irritability from lack of sleep. Stress takes on many forms; thus, we should try (myself included) to make sure we are taking care of our bodies and *speaking life* over our bodies so that we can be and do all that God has called us to be and do.

Scriptures:

*Now faith is the substance of things hoped for,
the evidence of things not seen.*
Hebrews 11:1 (KJV)

Let us hold fast to our profession(confession) of faith without wavering;(for he is faithful that promised).
Hebrews 10:23 (KJV)

For we walk by faith, not by sight.
2 Corinthians 5:7 (NKJV)

Life and death are in the power of the tongue.
Proverbs 18:21 (MSG)

Confession To Speak Life Always

Heavenly Father,

I thank you Lord for giving me the power to speak life into my life and into the lives of my children and those directly connected to me. Help me to keep a watch over my mouth and keep the doors of my lips so that I only say things that I want to see manifest in my life. I rebuke any idle, vain or contradicting words I may have spoken that go against what you have already spoken about me and my child(ren). I set myself up in agreement with you. Thank you, Lord, that I hold fast my confession of faith without wavering. God, I thank you that I live a life pleasing to you, for your word declares that without faith it is impossible to please you, Therefore, I choose to live a life of faith, to walk by faith and not by sight because I want to please you.

In Jesus Name,
Amen

CHAPTER 10
Single Mom Trusts God To Supply Her Needs

Whew, this one chapter can be a book right by itself, and ties in directly with our previous chapter. How many single women have been told or have had someone tell them they should get a sugar daddy to help them pay their bills? Or sleep with this one, or turn a few tricks here and there to make a dollar? Well, let me be the one to let you in on a little secret.... Are you ready?? The secret is...You don't have to! That's right, you don't have to depend on a man who may or may not come through for you, to meet your need. Someone may be reading this thinking, "Girl, you don't know all these bills I got. I can't pay these bills by myself. I have to keep sleeping with my boss so he can pad my paychecks with these bonuses." Or someone may be thinking, "Every two weeks, I have to rob Peter to pay Paul just to pay my essential bills." Well, let me challenge you to put an end to that cycle and learn to trust God to provide your needs. You save yourself from heartache, or having a man say, " Oh well, I did this and that for you, so you need to do so and so for me." No way, the last thing you want is to ask a sugar daddy to do a favor, then he turns around and says do "xyz", or holds it against you, or throws it back in your face and says, "Well, you wouldn't have this or that, if it weren't for me." Then he tries to control and manipulate you because he feels that since he gave you money or whatever, he has a say in your affairs. No ma'am!! Who has time for all that drama?? Again, God says, *He will supply all your needs according to His riches and glory.* The key is to use your faith as we discussed in the previous chapter, confess daily your confessions of faith, pray and trust God to supply your needs. Say, "God I thank You that all my needs are met and I have enough money to pay all my bills this month."

There have been countless times when I did not know how I was going to pay the full amount of a bill, and I just had more month than money. One time in particular, I did not know how I was going to pay my car payment. An emergency had come up that I had to handle and basically used my car payment money to handle the emergency situation. I didn't know what to do when it came time to pay my car payment. So I prayed, asked God and I talked to my mom or someone about it and they gave me the advice to call the bank and ask for a deferment on that month's payment. Well, I called the bank and, in my mind, I was thinking they probably won't work with me or they may give me a hard time. But I called anyway and spoke with the lady at the bank, I told her my situation and sure enough she granted me my request to have my car payment deferred for that month! That was nothing but the favor of God! And let me tell you this too, I was a tither; I honored God by giving Him back His ten percent.

Being a tither, you can claim God's protection (He will rebuke the devourer for your sake), you can claim God's provision (having resources provided to you that you need). God says, *prove me now if I will not open the windows of heaven and pour you out a blessing that won't be room enough to receive it* (Malachi 3:10). As a tither, having the favor of God working on your behalf and being able to claim God's protection and provision, you can't go wrong in life. Favor is God's way of allowing someone to use their power, their ability and their influence to help you. They may not understand their motivation, and they may say "I don't know why I'm doing this. Or they may say, "I/we don't normally do this but, for you..." We automatically know it's the *favor of God* moving for us on our behalf. The bible says in Psalm 5:12 that -*His Favor surrounds you as a shield*. Proverbs 21:1 helps us to understand that God can move on the hearts of man, to allow things to be worked in your favor! God has so many ways and people He can work through, to get to you what He wants you to have. It may not come the way I described in my situation, but just know God does not run out of options or ways on how to get things to you that are meant for you to receive. With God All things are possible. So, we must trust God (myself included) and believe that *now unto Him (God) who is able to do exceedingly abundantly above all we could ask or think, according to the power that works in us.* (Ephesians 3:20). I am reminded that God loves us, therefore, we can count on Him to see us through. He says He will never leave us nor forsake us. He is our Provider (Jehovah Jireh). He is always with us to see us through.

Scriptures:

I have been young and now am old, yet have I not seen the [uncompromisingly] righteous forsaken or their seed begging bread.
Psalm 37:25 (KJV)

Look at the birds of the air, that they do not sow, nor reap nor gather into barns, and yet your heavenly Father feeds them. Are you not worth much more than they?
Matthew 6:26 (NIV)

Both riches and honor come from you, and you rule over all, and in your hand is power and might; and it lies in your hand to make great and to strengthen everyone.
1 Chronicles 29:12 (NASV)

The Lord is my shepherd; I have everything I need [will lack nothing].
Psalm 23:1 (NCV)

For if you give, you will get! Your gift will return to you in full and overflowing measure, pressed down, shaken together to make room for more, and running over. Whatever measure you use to give, large or small, will be used to measure what is given back to you.
Luke 6:38 (KJV)

Confession To Trust God To Supply My Needs

Heavenly Father,

I thank you that you see me, you know where I am on this journey called life. Heavenly Father, as I come to you to make my needs known I thank you in advance for meeting my every need. I purpose in my heart to trust you more because you are my good shepherd, therefore, I lack nothing with you. I thank you that you know my needs before I even ask you. Thank you, Father, that I can come boldly to the throne of grace, that I may obtain mercy and find grace to help in time of need. Help me Father as I purpose in my heart to trust you more, not to lean and depend on man as my source, but to depend on you as my only source. For you are a God of plenty, a God of more than enough, therefore, I put my trust in you that you will supply all my needs according to your riches and glory in Christ Jesus.

In Jesus name,
Amen

Single Mom
NUGGET NOTES

CHAPTER 11
Single Mom and Her Prayer Life

What is prayer? Prayer is direct, one-to-one open communication or dialogue and interaction with God the Father through His son, Jesus Christ. A prayer life for anyone is so important. However, I can attest that a prayer life is very important, especially when you have little people and big people who are dependent on you to provide, feed, and guide them. So, who do you depend on then to help you? Give you strength? To carry the "Motherload"? To guide you, and give you wisdom to train up a child? Who do we turn to when things seem to be falling apart; crumbling right before our eyes? What do you do? Do you run to the phone? Run to your best friend? How often do we run to other people who may or may not have the answer to our problems? When times are hard and it seem like you don't know if you are coming or going, who do we run to? When you don't know how to handle little Johnny when he is acting up in school, or your teenager who lacks nothing has an attitude all the time and you can't understand why he is mad at the world, who do you run to?

During times when we just don't know, we reason within ourselves what the problem could be. Yet, reasoning doesn't help us understand what's really going on behind the scenes; that's when we can run to the ONE who knows what to do. We run to Him and sit at the feet of Jesus, and pour out ourselves before Him. He knows the answer to your problem before you even ask the question. He knows why little Johnny is acting a fool in school. He knows why your teenager is acting like he is. It is a privilege to be able to come boldly to the throne of grace. We can come to God boldly; come to His throne in prayer, not being timid or shy, and ask for His strength, His grace, and His power to help us to do what is it we need to do. God wants to help us through whatever we may face.

As I continue to grow in my walk with God, I am still grasping this reality myself as I always have had an independent mindset. So much so that if I want something done a certain way, I will do it myself and not ask for help because I know I can count on myself to get it done and not have to depend on anyone. When it comes to raising my son, I had the same mindset. A while ago, I had been dealing with some back-to-back issues and was completely stressed and worried, trying to figure things out on my own, when I heard God say, "You were never meant to carry this load by yourself." Wow, even in that moment God was like, "You are not alone, let me help you. this is not too hard for me to handle; let me work things out for you." God wants us to depend on Him. He does not want us to worry and be anxious; which is why the scripture tells us to come before him with prayer and thanksgiving and make our needs and wants known to God, and that is exactly what He desires of us. Someone reading this may ask, "Well, if God sees that I need help, why must I ask?" My response would be- it is because He is a gentleman; He will not force himself on you. Another time, I can remember when I was trying to figure out how a situation was going to work out. I finally got to the point where I was frustrated and I said, "Okay God, I'm not going to worry about this anymore. I am going to just let you deal with it!" I said it as if I was doing God a favor by saying, "Here God, you take it!" When in reality, that was what He wanted me to do from the beginning. I felt a huge relief after purposefully choosing to let go of the situation. The beautiful thing about prayer is, you can pray all throughout your day; while at work, at home, at school, or grocery shopping. Prayer can be as simple as, "Lord help me through this day." Prayer is not always being on your knees praying three hours straight every day. Now, don't get me wrong, everyone has their own way to pray. But, what I'm saying is, prayer can be short and sweet and God will still hear you.

I have seen times when the Lord even answered my *thoughts*. That was when I realized that our unspoken words are prayers, too. For example, my son who is very active and very involved in sports, happened to be gone to a track-and-field meet about two hours from where we lived. For whatever reason, I wasn't able to go. The team were traveling directly after school to this track-and-field meet while I was still at work, so I wasn't able to go. I have friends who I trust, who are the parents of my child's friend. It just so happens, our kids are on the same track-and-field team. This family also lives about ten minutes from our house; I remember thinking, it would be nice if my son could ride back home with them. I remember not wanting to impose and ask my friend if she could bring my son home with them, even though I knew she wouldn't have had any problem with my son riding back home with them. Now remember, this was just a thought I had; I cast it aside and I was like, "Well, I will just be prepared to get him from his school when it's time." Later on, I get a call from my son, and he says, "Mom, we are about to leave the track meet. My friend asked if it was okay for me to ride back home with them." It's a no-brainer what I said next. My answer was, "Yes", because these were the same friends who lived ten minutes from our house. I said all that to say that our thoughts are prayers too. God hears our thoughts, and without us even speaking a word, He answers them. Prayer is also a dialogue where we can listen to God and allow Him to speak to us and download wisdom, direction, and answers into our spirit. Listening is a very important form of communication in any relationship. When we listen to the voice of God, we can hear and receive His wisdom, know His desires and wants, and know the answers to the problems that we may face. God will help us to work through our problems.

Another form of prayer is speaking with other tongues, meaning you pray in your heavenly language or in the Holy Spirit. Jesus promised that after He left the world, that he would send the Holy Spirit. The Holy Spirit is our Counselor, Helper, Comforter, Strengthener, and Intercessor. Praying in the Holy Spirit is a very intimate prayer with God because praying in the Spirit is the Spirit interceding (intercessor) on your behalf to the Father and only the Father hears it and is able to interpret the prayer. See, when we pray out loud, in our normal language, the enemy hears it as well, and will try to put up blocks and decoys to hinder your prayers from being answered. Praying in the Spirit allows us to pray on another level, so to speak. When we pray in the spirit, we are praying for answers to problems we may be facing, or may face later down the road. The Holy Spirit will drop "it" into your spirit; providing the answer for what you were praying about. When praying in the Spirit, God reveals things. He makes things known to us that we wouldn't otherwise have known on our own. Being filled with the Holy Spirit, with the evidence of speaking in other tongues, is so powerful for any believer, whether single, married, widowed, or divorced.

You especially need God's supernatural on your natural, when it comes to the area of raising children. The Holy Spirit will tell you, or will give an unction that something may be going on with your child. If your child is trying to hide something, the Holy Spirit will reveal those things to you. As a mother, our mother's intuition kicks in when something isn't right with our children and we can pick up on it, if something is bothering them. Supporting our intuition, the Holy Spirit knows in-depth the details, and we can "tap into" what the Holy Spirit is revealing to us when we spend time praying in the spirit. Overall, prayer is a very important form of communication. Keeping the lines of communication open with our Heavenly Father by praying daily is so beneficial. It helps us to keep up our courage and to not turn into cowards who give up, faint, and lose heart. (Luke 18:1).

Scriptures:

The earnest prayer of a righteous person has great power and produces wonderful results.
James 5:16b **(NLT)**

However, when He, the Spirit of truth, has come, He will guide you into all truth; for He will not speak on His own authority, but whatever He hears He will speak; and He will tell you things to come.
John 16:13 **(NLT)**

Be anxious for nothing, but in everything by prayer and supplication, with thanksgiving, let your requests be made known to God.
Philippians 4:6 **(NJV)**

Then you will call upon Me and go and pray to Me, and I will listen to you.
Jeremiah 29:12 **(NKJV)**

But you, when you pray, go into your room, and when you have shut your door, pray to your Father who is in the secret place; and your Father who sees in secret will reward you openly.
Matthew 6:6 **(NKJV)**

My sheep hear My voice, and I know them, and they follow Me.
John 10:27 **(NKJV)**

Confession Over Prayer Life

Father,

I thank you when I pray, I know that you hear me whatever I may ask according to your will, I know that I have the petitions that I desire of you. I thank you Father that I am your sheep and you are my shepherd, therefore I know your voice and I hear you clearly when you speak answers to me. The voice of a stranger I will not follow. Thank you Father, that my prayers do not fall on deaf ears, but that you hear me when I pray. I thank you that you have given me my heart's desires and have not withheld the request from my lips.

In Jesus Name,

Amen.

CHAPTER 12
Our Children, Our Blessing, Our Future

Helping our children recognize their God-given talents and maximize their full potential to succeed

In the United States, Mother's Day was first celebrated by Anna Jarvis in 1907 when she held a memorial of her mother. Mother's Day was later signed into an official holiday in 1914 by President Woodrow Wilson. However, Mother's Day has been a major holiday that has been celebrated in the world for centuries. Anna Jarvis trademarked the phrase, "Second Sunday in May, Mother's Day" to give special honor to mothers. We celebrate and honor our mothers in many different ways, including but not limited to going out to eat. Waiting in long lines to get Momma into her favorite restaurant to eat her favorite meal. Mother's Day always falls on a Sunday, therefore you can bet on seeing the Mothers of the church coming out in their vibrant church suits with matching, large, colorful hats and matching shoes and pocketbooks. Mother's Day is a very special occasion, and we can look at it as a gift that God has given us, because without our children, fostered or adopted, we would not be able to celebrate this special day. Children are a gift from God. Psalm 127:3 says, *"No doubt children are a gift from the Lord.*

The fruit of the womb is a divine reward." God saw fit and entrusted us to take care of what is His. When God made our children, He created them special, and put seeds of greatness in them. Our job as a mother, and as temporary stewards of our children, is to make sure they grow up healthy, and strong in the things of God. We want them to grow in stature as Jesus did; having favor with God and man.

When we observe our children growing, we take notice of the things our children have a natural "bent" towards, meaning what their natural talents and gifts are. More than likely, these will be what they have a natural bent towards in life, or possibly their purpose is related to their particular "bent". God has put seeds of greatness in each one of our children related to that "bent." As parents, we must help our children to grow in the potential related to their natural "bent". For instances, if you notice your child has a "bent", or a gift, talent and interest at a young age for playing drums, then their gifts and talents may be in music. As a parent, you can help expand their gifts and talents by signing them up for drum lessons, or have them play in a band, or be a part of the music ministry in church, playing drums. If you notice your child has a knack for baking, and loves being in the kitchen baking and cooking, then it could be that possibly the "bent" God has for them is in the area of culinary arts. So how can you help your child become stronger in that area that you notice they have an interest in? You can help strengthen and expand their potential by signing them up for baking classes, buying cookbooks and keeping them around the house to let them try new recipes, or letting them create their own their own recipes and preparing the creative dishes. You can have them watch food networks and food channels where they can pick up on tips for baking in the kitchen. If you notice your child likes doing things with their hands; putting things together and taking things apart, then they may have a natural "bent" towards the engineering field, creating and building things, or carpentry. If you notice your child has a bible in their hand and pretends to be preaching to a congregation filled with stuffed animals and dolls, your child may have a "bent" towards ministry in the pulpit.

The bible talks about how when Jesus was twelve years old, he went with his family to Jerusalem every year for the Passover feast. One day he stayed behind in Jerusalem. His parents were worried; they didn't know where he was. They frantically backtracked to Jerusalem and they found him sitting in the temple among teachers, listening to them and asking questions. The bible talks about how the teachers were impressed with the sharpness of Jesus' answers. Let me remind you, He was only twelve at the time. However, his parents weren't impressed at all; they were just frightened and upset. His mother was upset and asked him, "Why have you done this to us? Your father and I have been out of our minds looking for you." And Jesus replied, "Why were you looking for me"? Didn't you know I had to be here dealing with the things of my father?" The bible says Jesus' parents had no idea what He was talking about. So even at 12 years old, Jesus had a natural "bent" toward ministry. He knew He was to be about His Father's business. If his mother and father had picked up on Jesus' "bent" to what God had put in Him, they would not have been upset about the fact that he stayed behind in the temple. This story is found in Luke 2:41-52.

Helping our children expand in their abilities, exposing them to what their "bent" is towards, and strengthening them in those areas could potentially help them grow into their God-given gifts. Your intentional support may help them t find their purpose early in life and enable them to walk and grow in their purpose at a young age. When I was a young mother, working as a certified nursing assistant, I was telling one of my patients about my son; he was maybe three or four years old at the time. My patient gave me a piece of good advice, especially coming from a male perspective, he said to keep him active in church and sports to keep him out of trouble. When we keep our children active in church, they learn the things of God. This spiritual training is so important as our children grow into adults. They will know what it means to have a relationship with Jesus. "Train up a child in the way he should go and when he is old, he will not depart from it" (Proverb 22: 6). Keeping our children active in sports helps them learn team building skills, how to play fair, how to play well and get along with others, and how to listen to instruction and follow rules. It teaches our children discipline and good sportsmanship which can carry over and positively influence other areas in a child's life. In these last days, God says He will pour out His spirit on all flesh, your sons and daughters will prophesy. God can use babes and children as vessels to speak through, to get his word out, and to break things in the spirit.

Therefore, we must not look down on young children, but edify and build them up. They are our future.

Scriptures:

A man's gift makes room for him, and brings him before great men.
Proverbs 18:16 (NKJV)

His seed shall be mighty upon the earth: the generation of the upright shall be blessed.
Proverbs 112:2 (NKJV)

But He said, "Leave the children alone, and do not forbid them from coming to Me; for the kingdom of heaven belongs to such as these
Matthew 19:14 (NKJV)

For I know the thoughts that I think towards you says the Lord, thoughts of peace and not of evil, to give you a future and a hope.
Jeremiah 29:11 (NKJV)

Confession Over Child's God-given Talents

I thank you, Lord for giving me an eye to see the gifts and talents you have placed in my child(ren). Thank you for giving me creative ideas and ways to bring out and enhance my child(ren)'s gifts and talents. Thank you, Lord, that my child(ren) will become and grow close to you as he explores the depth of his calling, plan, and purpose for his life. I thank you for the right exposure needed for my child(ren) to develop and perfect the gifts you've given him. Father God, I thank you for giving my child(ren) the confidence and boldness he needs to operate in his gift and to be used as your vessel here in the earth, for your will and your glory,

In Jesus Name,
Amen

Single Mom
NUGGET NOTES

CHAPTER 13
Setting Your Child Up in the Right Educational Environment to Flourish, Thrive and Succeed!

There is no secret that each individual child is totally different when it comes to learning. Each child has a different response to learning styles, and I firmly believe that you can't put all children in one basket and expect them to all learn the same way and at the same speed. Some children catch on quickly, then you have other children who need repetition in order to learn a skill set. And parents, that is perfectly okay! This does not always mean that something is wrong with your child. Thus, I believe the need for diverse and creative ways of making learning fun in the classroom setting is absolutely essential to the academic advancement of our children. I believe the opposite is also true. If you have a teacher who focuses on instruction only, and the students, early elementary-aged children, have to be still, quiet, and cannot talk or move, as if they are in a college classroom setting, then ultimately you are setting some of your children up to fail. Children who are five and six years of age are inquisitive; they like to explore and typically learn things hands-on. Therefore, it is possible that a child's creativity and learning style can be suppressed to the point where a child's grades suffer horribly. In addition, the child may lose interest in learning because of ineffective teaching methods that are not compatible with the learning style of the student. However, I believe this same child can be effectively taught when their learning style is discovered and teaching methods can be adapted to best fit the learning style of that student. Thus in turn, you will see a positive outcome in your student's grades and it can possibly heighten their drive to want to learn; making it easier for the them to absorb and retain information taught to them. Now, don't get me wrong. There are some excellent teachers out there who deserve a gold medal and who stand behind and back their students 100%, and are committed to helping their students succeed. And to be honest, it makes the school year so much better when you have a good teacher you can partner with to help your child academically. However, just like in any profession, there are some bad apples in the barrel. You may have some teachers who you may question, "Why did you become a teacher in the first place?" I mean really, let's be honest here. Some may be tired, and possibly experiencing burnout. If that is the case, then it would help everyone if they would just kindly remove themselves or take a sabbatical. As a parent, is it very important that we learn our children's teaching style. That way, when parent-teacher meetings are being held, we can collaborate with the teachers to assist them in helping our children reach their full academic potential.

For my single parents, I also believe that it is important starting early on, when your child is in early elementary school, to be active and present for everything going on with your child in school-related activities. I consider early elementary as grades K-2nd grade. Being proactive will help you keep up with how well your child is doing in school. It's "okay" to check up on your child and email the teacher and ask how your child is progressing in school. Especially if it has been a while since you have heard anything from your child's teacher about your child's progress in school. Staying on top of things early, will allow you as a parent, to keep your child from falling through the cracks and possibly being left behind if your child is not fully comprehending the material being taught. This also builds a rapport with your child's teacher and you can partner with your child's teacher to help your child succeed in the classroom.

Another reason why being proactive in your child's schooling, checking assignments, and staying on top of things, including regular, direct communication with the teacher is so important, is because unfortunately, it is during the early stages of school when children are "labeled" by teachers. When I say "labeled", I mean that some teachers have already made up their mind about your child's ability or inability to learn and if your child will make it through school or not. Unfortunately, this "label" given to your child by some teachers, typically stays with your child as records of your child are passed down from grade to grade, with your child having a reputation following them based on what another teacher has said. Which means your child never gets an opportunity to be looked at through "fresh lenses", without having judgement already passed on them before the next teacher can know them personally. Which is unfair to the child. This is also a time when some teachers will say your child has learning disabilities, or other teachers will deem your child as "exceptional" and unable to learn beyond basic skills. Thus not giving your child a fair chance at being taught like other students. Also, some teachers will say your child needs to be on medication and will try to say your child has ADD or ADHD. This is most commonly seen with African American, and Hispanic children who have already been labeled by society as demonstrating poor performance in school. Yes, some Caucasian children are labeled as well, but this is most commonly seen among minority students. As a result, our minority students are placed on individualized education plans (IEPs) or 504-plans, without parents even being aware. Which is why it is essential to stay on top of your child's daily school work, and consistently communication with your child's teachers.

If you find out the teacher has your child on a plan, then tells you your child has a learning disability, it can be stressful. Especially when you haven't seen any signs of your child having any learning disabilities, and your child seems to follow directions and learn well at home. I would advise you not to completely take the teacher's word for it. I am not bashing teachers; they are great pillars in our society. However, while they can give expertise on teaching, they are not experts on medical diagnoses. I would recommend you make an appointment with your child's pediatrician if there is really a concern. Have your pediatrician tell you what to do from there. Your child's pediatrician may want to do testing on your child or other assessments required by a medical professional. I would inquire with my child's doctor before agreeing with the teacher that your child needs medication. Unfortunately, medications like the most commonly used drug, Ritalin, comes with many side effects and may alter your child's mood and behaviors, causing them to be sluggish and impeding their ability to learn in the classroom. In my own personal experience with my child, he was in first grade when his teacher told me that my child was on an IEP program and that he needed to be on medication for ADD or ADHD. Then she tried to justify it by saying that her daughter was on medication. Let me tell you, I did not accept what this teacher was saying; I respectfully disagreed with her. Why? First of all, because I knew my child. He would sit still and quiet anywhere, and I would always get compliments on how his manners and well-behaved he was when out in public. Secondly, I knew a lady whose child really suffered from ADD, and my child was not displaying any of those signs of ADD or ADHD. I spoke with others in my family, and outside of my family who were educators to seek more advice. I even dropped in on my son's class time, just to watch and observe how he was acting in class. I wanted to check his behaviors, and if my son was doing all the things the teacher was saying he was doing. I did not let my child or the teacher know that I would be coming to sit in on the class. My child did not know that I was observing him when I was in the classroom. What I observed was my child participating and sitting on his rear-end like the other students, answering questions raising his hand, and being participatory. He followed directions and he was not loud, rude, or being "a busy body". Sometimes to you have to see for yourself, and what I saw was totally different from what his teacher was trying to make him out to be. That year was a very trying year, as this teacher had singled out my child that entire school year for petty things, and I constantly stayed at the school for little things that I did not agree with that she had done. I also scheduled a parent-teacher meeting with the principle present, just to maintain rapport with this teacher so that my child could be in a learning environment that was fair to him. For my child loved school, and was very eager to learn. I saw that in him and I was determined and made sure that no one would ruin my child's ambition and his drive to learn. Unfortunately, so many students are not being given a fair opportunity to learn. Either they are being suspended or spend too much time in in-school suspension (ISS)for small, petty things, thus decreasing their time spent in the classroom which puts them further behind in learning.

Some of you may have heard of the school-prison pipeline. If not, what is it? Poor educational experiences pushes students to the streets and then funnels students to one- way paths to prison. Thus, these various policies referred to as the school-to-prison pipeline pushes children out of school through excessive suspensions. African American and Hispanic children are more likely to be suspended than their peers. When children are being suspended out of school, not only do they miss class time, but they also fall behind in their school work, making it difficult for them to catch up. Constant suspensions and ISS, use of in-school officers, and other factors, all contribute to the school-prison pipeline theory. I believe as single mothers, we really have a part to play to make sure our children are not falling into the school-prison pipeline and thus becoming a statistic. By being involved in our children's affairs in the school setting and assisting and supporting our children, we can prevent this. When a parent is not involved, it lessens the child's chance for success. Especially if the student is experiencing situation after situation with their teacher, and just can't seem to catch a break even though the student may have a desire to do well in school. The student could very well be being "picked on", and constantly called out for petty things by the teacher, and the parents may think that it's the child when in actuality, if the parents dig a little deeper, there's more to it. Now, I'm not saying this is the case for all students, but it is definitely the case for some. A research study shows that minorities were more likely to be suspended from school than those who weren't minorities. I later found out that this same teacher I had trouble with, had a history of singling out African American males in her classroom.

Now, I said all that. However, let me point out the other side of this discussion. If you do notice that you child is having some issues, and what the teacher is saying about your child is true, and you can see the signs, I encourage you to take heed. I would still follow through with my child seeing their pediatrician to get my child the help they need to be successful academically. In any situation, changing your child's environment to best accommodate their needs can be vital when it comes to your child's learning. Placing your child in an environment that is conducive to learning is very important to help your child succeed. You may find that your child does not do well in large classroom settings, but you find that they excel in smaller classroom settings. You may notice that your child thrives in more advanced classes that challenge them and they are bored in classes that do not challenge them. You may find that your child does better in a magnet school, charter school, private school, or when home-schooled. There are many schools to be researched in finding the school that best fits your child. Please know that to find the best match for your child may require trial-and-error. However, you want your child in an environment that is conducive to learning and that best fits their needs. Seek out the environment which will cause them to thrive and excel academically. An environment that increases their chances of obtaining a high school diploma and advancing to a career, occupation or obtaining a skill set that is fulfilling to them. Ultimately, be guided by the Lord; pray and seek His face about any matters of the heart concerning your children. Ask Him for wisdom and clear direction about what is best for your children.

Scriptures for Wisdom:

Plans are established by seeking advice; so if you wage war, obtain guidance.
Proverbs 20:18 (NIV)

If any of you lacks wisdom, you should ask God, who gives generously to all without finding fault, and it will be given to you.
James 1:5 (NIV)

For the Lord grants wisdom! From his mouth come knowledge and understanding. He grants a treasure of common sense to the honest. He is a shield to those who walk with integrity. He guards the paths of the just and protects those who are faithful to him. Then you will understand what is right, just, and fair, and you will find the right way to go.
Proverbs 2:6-9 (NLT)

The beginning of wisdom is: get Wisdom (skillful and godly Wisdom)! (For skillful and godly Wisdom is the principal thing.) And with all you have gotten , get understanding(discernment, comprehension, and interpretation).
Proverbs 4:7 (AMPC)

Confession for Divine Placement of a Multitude of Counsels

Jesus,

Your word says that if anyone lacks wisdom, to ask of Him who gives generously. So Lord, I come to you to ask you for wisdom, clear direction, understanding and guidance in my situation (be specific what the situation is in your life). I believe I receive Godly wisdom to make right choices as the parent/guardian of the child(ren) you've given me to raise and I have boldness and am obedient to your promptings in the way in which you tell me to go. I thank you Lord for placing people in my path who can also help lead me and direct me, for your word declares that in a multitude of counselors there is safety. (Prov 11:14 KJV) Thank you, Lord, that you are also concerned about the small matters of my heart that concern me.

In Jesus Name,
Amen

CHAPTER 14
Single Mom Secures the Bag!

When it comes to securing the bag, and making that money; get them coins! There are many barriers to employment that single mothers face in the United States. These barriers include finding affordable child care, and work schedules that accommodate their needs. Having a sick child, or a flat tire can mean a lost job. According to a New York Times analysis of current population survey data, the number of single mothers in the work force has climbed since 2015 by about four percentage points. Also, jobs in nursing and in managing of inventory in warehouses showed the highest growth of employment for young single mothers between 2015 and 2018. *Securing the bag* can look like so many things, like doing hair on the side, or babysitting someone's kids, or selling plates to earn extra income for your family. *Securing the bag* can also come from monies from yearly tax returns or Pell Grant checks that come in if you are in school. When my son was younger, and I was working a low-end paying job, I greatly benefited from my yearly tax refund money. I mean, I went spending crazy! I also would receive money from a Pell Grant that I was able to use towards things that assisted me with school, like gas and school supplies. But back then, I was in a different mindset. I was not thinking about future financial investments and gains. I wasn't thinking to save some of the couple thousands I got back every year from tax returns, or a couple hundred I received from financial aid assistance. At a younger age, I just did not have the mindset to save up to buy a house or to invest, or to set aside money for my son to have and to let it earn interest without touching it. If I had the mindset I have now, back then, I would be sitting real pretty with stacked up money in the bank and I would possibly be in my second or third house by now. I wish someone would have told me.

So, I would like to pass this advice on to my younger, single mothers who receive thousands of dollars per child from tax returns. Spend your money wisely. Think about your future. Set up goals; visualize where you see yourself with your children five years from where you are now. A lot can happen in five years. Would you like to own a home? How about saving up money to pay cash for a car instead of taking out a loan? Consider the money you need to invest in your child(ren)'s future; your kids may go to college. When you receive lump sums of money at one time, put some money aside every year that you can't touch and allow it to earn interest so that your child(ren) will start off with a nice lump sum of money he/she can have access to when she/he turns eighteen.

Some people think that getting a credit card will solve any money problems they may have. But that is far from the truth if it is used incorrectly. Don't think running up a credit card is the thing to do. Unfortunately, a credit card can really put you in a pile of debt, especially if the interest rates on the credit is outrageously high, and you are not paying your payments on time. When the use of a credit card is abused, credit cards can be a disaster and ruin your credit rating, which will continue to show on your credit reports for up to seven years. A low credit score can hinder your ability to get approved for a loan of any kind, it can also prevent you from taking advantage of low interest rates and other perks. When you have bad credit, the creditors see you as a "risk"; meaning they see how you lack the ability to pay your bills on time. However, if a credit card is used responsibly, and is paid off on time, and you keep your utilization rate low on the credit cards, it can help raise your credit score. This will place you in a better position to buy a house with low interest rates, without having to pay mortgage insurance. Having good credit can give you the ability to drive a fully equipped, new car right off the car lot!

Dave Ramsey who is a personal finance guru is known for the famous seven step guide to save money, pay off debt, and build wealth. However, I will just touch on the first step of his baby-step process. The very first step of Dave Ramsey's seven step guide is to have an emergency fund of one thousand dollars saved. As a single mom, I believe having an emergency fund is very important, as unexpected expenses may come up, such as needing a new set of tires, appliances may breakdown, or we may need new parts for our cars. There have been plenty of times, as I look back, when I was able to get one thousand dollars easily, just by being a recipient of and taking advantage of (not abusing) the various programs out there that assist single mothers with dependents. Having that cushion of one thousand dollars or more saved, can give you a peace of mind, knowing that if some unexpected expenses were to pop up, you don't have to be stressed out about how to find the money to cover the expense.

Studies have shown that 22% of Americans experience extreme stress from finances. Having a short term and long-term financial goal is just as important as any other goal. I believe the key is to start small and build yourself up. Create a budget for yourself and stick with it, if you get off track, it's not the end of the world; just get back on track and begin again, or pick up where you left off. If you are able, consult with a financial advisor to help you with budgeting tasks. Then as your income increases, your ability to save more will also increase. As you see your account growing and your hard work paying off, you will be proud and have a sense of accomplishment. Remember that God blessed you to be able to make the extra monies to save, and to ultimately be a blessing to others. Being a blessing financially to someone else who may have a need, puts you in position to receive an even greater blessing. Don't think you have to do something huge to be a blessing to others. Sometimes blessing someone with something that seems small to you, could be a big gesture and blessing for someone else. Most importantly, on a daily basis, allow God to use you and direct you on who to bless and how to meet their need. The ability to be in good standing financially so you can bless others, is a great feeling. Especially if you see other single mothers experiencing difficulties and going through some of the same obstacles that you yourself have already gone through and overcome. Financial stability puts you in a position to be a blessing to someone else.

Scriptures

He who is faithful in a very little thing is also faithful in much.
Luke 16:10 (AMP)

Wealth obtained by fraud dwindles, but he who gathers by (honest) labor will increase (his riches).
Proverbs 13:11 (AMP)

The Blessing of the Lord makes one rich, and he add forth no sorrow with it.
Proverbs 10:22 (NKJV)

Let them shout for joy and be glad, Who favor my righteous cause; And let them say continually, "Let the Lord be magnified, Who has pleasure in the prosperity of His servant".
Psalm 35:27 (NKJV)

Wealth and riches will be in his house, and his righteousness endures forever.
Psalm 112:3 (NKJV)

Confession Over My Finances

Father,

I thank you for giving me the power and the ability to get wealth, I thank you for blessing me with the knowledge, wisdom, creative ideas, witty inventions that will allow me to increase in monies so that I can be a blessing in the kingdom of God and to others. Thank you for giving me Godly wisdom and strategies to being a good steward and to remain faithful over the little, so that you can increase me to being faithful over much, and to bless others as you instruct me to, and I will give you all the glory, honor, and praise

In Jesus Name,
Amen

CHAPTER 15
Crushing Your Goals, Working Nine to Five, and Raising Children IS Possible!

When the majority of your time is spent raising children, or being a guardian for children that you may have "inherited", it is so easy to get wrapped up in being a caregiver. Our role becomes cheering our children on to follow their dreams and aspirations, and we tend to forget the dreams and aspirations we once had. We tend to put ourselves on the back burner, and we forget the very things that made our heart smile; the very things we had love and passion for, and we once imagined doing. After a while, those dreams and ambitions seem dead, and we may feel like they cannot be resurrected. Maybe life's circumstances cause you to believe your dreams and desires are out of reach. However, if these dreams and desires were once in your heart, I believe that they are still in your heart. Because ultimately, the desires you have come from God. God imparted seeds of greatness into your life, and as you walk closer to Him, He begins to prune you. God begins to water the seeds of greatness He placed in you. These seeds of greatness begin to grow to full-term. Then when the time is right, this greatness will be birthed through you, and from you. When these desires have laid dormant for a long time, God has to stir those desires up in you again, so that you can fulfill and bring those desires into manifestation. Ultimately, these are the desires He put in you. Lately you may not have had a stirring to do anything, so just ask God to stir up in you any dreams that you have let die because you may have thought it was too late. Another thing to remember is that a delay is not a denial. Some people have allowed their dreams and visions to die because they think that because it didn't happen when they wanted it to happen, meant that it wasn't meant to happen. But, I challenge you to ask God to show you those things that you let die. Ask Him to resurrect, or "stir" up those things, and breathe on those things which you thought were dead, and make them alive again. You can work your regular nine-to-five and come home, and work on building a family business. Some may say, 'I have not been able to tackle those things that I once set out to do because there is not enough time or hours in a day". Some may say, "I don't have the energy". Some may go home and flop on the couch to take a nap; exhausted from being in the office all day dealing with rude customers over the phone, as they cursed you out over a debt you were trying to collect. Or you may be exhausted from repetitive physical labor from your eight hour day. Whatever the case may be, I'm here to tell you that you can work your regular nine-to-five, take care of your kids, and still have time to work on your dreams and ambitions. You may ask, "Well, how do I do that? I am not super woman! When will I have time to rest?"

We all have dreams, desires and ambitions that I believe God has placed in us for a reason. "So, how do I get my vision from out of the invisible into the visible?", you ask. First of all, take it to God in prayer; get clear understanding and direction on what it is He wants you to do. Then I would encourage you to read *Habakkuk 2:2* that says to *"write the vision, and make it plain"*. We need to write down the vision so that we can work toward making it tangible. Next, write down the goals, and give yourself a reasonable deadline to work towards achieving each goal. Small advancements turn into big advancements overtime. You may not be able to take on things by leaps and bounds, but starting slow is better than not starting at all. Let's say you want to go back to school to be a registered nurse. Being specific about what you are going after is important when working towards manifesting your dreams and desires. Thankfully, a lot of diploma and degree programs can be obtained by taking online courses and do not require that you be in a classroom setting. Thus, giving you more flexibility on when you can schedule your classes and get your assignments completed; all from the comfort of your own home. If taking one on-line class a semester is all you can do, then do that. Just because you aren't able to handle a full twelve or more credit hours a semester doesn't mean you aren't making progress. Start small and work your way up. As long as you are moving forward, that is considered progress.

Another thing that helps is to create a vision board. What I have done in the past, was to create a vision board by cutting out pictures from magazines or newspapers, and cutting out words that spelled out what I wanted to achieve. I then used these items to create my vision board. I took a picture of my completed vision board and placed it as a screen saver on my phone, so that every time I turn on my phone, my vision is the first thing I see. It helps keep things into perspective and reminds me of my goals. (Shout out to Steve Harvey for that idea.) I also have my vision board up in my room where I can see it, to be reminded daily of my goals so that I don't lose sight of what I'm working towards. Having your vision board in plain sight is very important, as it serves as a reminder of what you are striving for. Have you ever heard of the saying, "out of sight out of mind"? That is what we want to avoid. If you want to keep your goals in your mind, and be focused on where you are going, keeping your vision board in plain sight is beneficial.

Working on your goals and perfecting your craft can be achieved after leaving your nine-to-five, and after you come home, get the children straightened out, and get yourself refreshed with a hot shower and a brief nap. Then, get back up and spend an hour or two working towards your vision, while the house is quiet and you can focus without any distractions. When you start to work towards something you feel passionate and strongly about, and you find yourself constantly thinking about that specific thing, the work becomes enjoyable instead of work that you dread. If you are not careful, you may find yourself being up for hours, late into the night because you are driven by your passion and its' purpose. You may find yourself spending more time without even realizing it because it's a joy and not drudgery. When you begin to notice that you are meeting your set goals, that also fuels your energy to keep going; for you see your vision and dreams moving closer to becoming a reality.

Scriptures:

And so I am sure confident that God, who began this good work in you, will carry it on until it is finished on the day of Christ Jesus
Philippians 1:6 (NKJV)

Roll your works upon the Lord (commit and trust them wholly to Him; He will cause your thoughts to become agreeable to His will, and) so shall your plans be established and succeed.
Proverbs 16:3 (NKJV)

For the vision is yet for the appointed (future) time it hurries toward the goal (of fulfillment) it will not fail. Even though it delays, wait(patiently) for it, because it will certainly come; it will not delay.
Habakkuk 2:3 (NKJV)

But Jesus looked at them and said to them" With men this is impossible, but with God all things are possible".
Matthew 19:26 (NKJV)

Confession For Fulfillment of God's Plan and Purpose Over My Life

Father God,

I thank you for all the plans and purposes you have for my life, I thank you Father that you have begun a good work in me, I commit my plans to you God and I ask that you be Lord over all that I put my hands to do. Lord, stir up in me the visions, goals, dreams that you have placed in me that I may have given up on. Resurrect those dreams that I have let die and give me a fresh perspective, fresh anointing, and fresh start, that I may find new hope to work towards, fulfilling the God-given desires that have been placed in me, So that it may succeed and prosper and so that you will get the glory for it in the end.

In Jesus Name,
Amen

Single Mom
NUGGET NOTES

CHAPTER 16
Keeping Your Child Engaged in Community Events

I distinctly remember when I was working as a certified nursing assistant, that one of my patients advised me to keep my son in sports and in church. The patient stressed that it was very important. Then, being my 20-year-old self, and not having a mature mindset, it did not dawn on me why he would say that. However, as my male child has grown up in age, keeping him active in sports was very good for him. Being an only child, my son did not have to worry about sharing toys or interact with other children in our home. Involvement in sports kept him busy, and he learned to be a team-player, and to work with other kids. Sports taught my son, team-building skills and discipline.

Keeping your child active in sports allows the child to interact with other children their age. It also allows your child to discover themselves in athletics and helps them determine what they like and don't like. At a young age, a lot of children may start out in various sports such as tee ball, soft ball, soccer, gymnastics, or cheerleading, which are great sports and can help develop your child's character, strengths and abilities. Sports can also help increase a child's sense of responsibility early, when they understand that they play a part that help makes the team successful. Sports like taekwondo and karate, can help develop discipline and inner strength and teach respect which goes a long way in the home setting when you have asked little Johnny to do something, and instead of little Johnny talking back, little Johnny applies the principles he has learned in karate and taekwondo and says, "Yes, ma'am" and performs the task quickly and with care. This can make home life easier and less frustrating because little Johnny has learned the importance of being obedient and respectful when spoken to by an adult. Keeping your child active in some sport will increase your child's self-esteem and give your child a sense of accomplishment and something to be proud of. It will also make you a proud mommy when you see your child demonstrating exceptional strengths and abilities in areas you never thought your child had. Now, you are proud and you find yourself bragging on how awesome your child is in their skills.

If you are a single mom, I would highly recommend finding a church home and asking God if it is right for you and your family. Then I would recommend being "active" in church. "Active" in church means serving in your church. It could be singing in the choir, ushering, having your child participate in programs specifically tailored for the youth; it could be quoting a bible verse, or putting on a skit. This helps our children learn to serve in the house of God. Also, by learning about the things of God, and being around other peers who have a common belief in God, your child will be less likely to give in to peer pressure or try to "fit in" with the wrong crowd; a crowd, that as a parent you really wouldn't want your child to try to "fit in" to. When your child enjoys going to church because they love the youth department and find good, solid friends, that is a plus! I'm reminded of the scripture that says, *"iron sharpens iron"*. Just like any good parent, you want to see your child associate with good friends. Raising your child in a church environment, can also help them to learn principles they can carry with them into everyday life. Your child will know how to pray and handle the life situations they may face at school or outside of school in a manner that is pleasing to God. Involvement in church can help improve the home life, and back up the foundations and morals you instill in your child in the home setting. Having your child in church can lead to the development and enhancement of leadership skills, and create a good moral foundation that your child will take with them wherever they go. They can apply these principles in the home setting, the classroom setting, and even in the workplace setting (for our teenagers).

In my experience as a single mom, having my child grow up in church has impacted him greatly. Being a single mom, he does not have the godly male figure example in the home. However, our church has a class specifically for our young boys called the "Courage Class". In it, my pastor, Dr. Bernard Grant, is able to get with the boys on their level and teach them and pour into them from not only just a male perspective, but also from a godly, male perspective. Dr. Grant teaches the uncompromising word of God to help equip our teens to grow from boyhood to manhood. In the Courage Class, he teaches them how to accept responsibility, and the danger of not controlling their anger (a lot of grown men have this issue today because of father issues or growing up without having a father in the home). Dr. Grant teaches the class from a biblical perspective, while providing relevant examples for applying the principles learned. Which has been a sheer blessing for my son. The Courage Class could not have come at a better time for my son, as he is in his early teen years. He is at the age when he is still navigating through this thing called life. He is at a time when he is going through puberty, and his body is changing and different emotions and mood swings are occurring at this time of any teenager's life. The Courage Class came at the most pivotal and crucial point in my son's life; to support his growth, development and character from boyhood into young adulthood. And for that I'm forever grateful.

My son also participates in ushering in our church, on the first Sunday of every month. He is part of the Junior Ushers. The Junior Ushers seat the church attendees in their chairs, they are uniformed and everything is done *decent and in order*. So, for my son, ushering teaches him how to serve others, it teaches order, it teaches him how to be use good manners, it teaches chivalry (which has been long gone), and it teaches respect. In addition, ushering teaches my son how to receive correction and the importance of having a teachable spirit as he takes instructions from the adult male ushers who are "overseers" of the Junior Ushers. Being a member of the Junior Ushers also helps him to see first-hand the example of good, godly male role models in the church. Having come from a family filled with preachers and ministers on my mom side, going to church was instilled into me at an early age. I didn't like it when I was younger, but now that I'm older hindsight is always 20/20, and I'm grateful for having come from a strong family with strong faith and belief in God. We are to *train up a child in the way he should go, and when he is old, he will not depart from it.*(Proverb 22: 6. NKJV) Some reading this may say, "Well, I brought my child up in church and now they are grown and acting a fool out here in these streets!" Well, I believe that they will come to their senses and will be drawn back in to what they were taught. In the meantime, continue to pray for your child's protection while they are doing their thing (apart from the things of God) and that their eyes will be opened and that God will place someone in their path to redirect them back to having a relationship with God. Teaching our children early on, to have a servant's heart and attitude and to live by the foundation of Jesus, will always be in them. So even if they stray, it is instilled in them, and when they decide to have a serious relationship with Jesus, they will come back to Him.

Keeping your child busy in community activities such as church and sports, keeps them busy and decreases their chances of engaging with the wrong crowds and picking up bad habits that could land them in a juvenile detention center or jail. Having your child involved in these activities will help you to raise a well-rounded individual who can take the principles they learn from a coach or pastor or any other significant pillar of the community and apply the principles to their lives. In turn, this will make your home life easier and create well-rounded adults who will one day become the pillars in their communities who will have the opportunity to pour into and reach those coming up behind them. Each one reach one!

Scriptures

People were also bringing babies to Jesus for him to place his hands on them. When the disciples saw this, they rebuked them. But Jesus called the children to him and said "Let the little children come to me, and do not hinder them, for the kingdom of God belongs to such as these.
Luke 18:15-16 (NIV)

All your children will be taught by the Lord, and great will be their peace.
Isaiah 54:13 (NIV)

And Jesus matured, growing up in both body and spirit, blessed by both God and people.
Luke 2:52 (MSG)

Train up a child in the way he should go, And when he is old he will not depart from it.
Proverbs 22:6 (NKJV)

Confession For God To Give Me Spiritual Leaders After HIS Own Heart

Heavenly Father,

I thank you for providing me with a spiritual leader/pastor. One whom my kids and I can grow and learn from, who will teach the uncompromising word of God in simplicity and in truth. I thank you Lord, that all my children are taught of the Lord and great is their peace. Father God, I thank you for helping me to be the example in the home of what it looks like to have a close relationship with you (Jesus), help me to teach of your ways to my children, that they may grow in the Lord and develop their own personal relationship with you. Father God, I thank you that my children have an attitude of servanthood to serve others just as Christ did. I pray my child(ren) grow (mature in stature) and that they have favor with God and man. I pray that they will let their light shine and show the love of God to all others they may come in contact with.

In Jesus Name,
Amen

CHAPTER 17
Single Mom Networks

What is the definition of *network*? *Network* is defined as *interaction with others to exchange information to develop professional and social contacts*. Networking with other single mothers has benefits. Networking provides the opportunity for you to be able to socialize and interact with other single mothers who have similar responsibilities and interests that you may have. Starting a networking group on a social media page or creating a blog for single mothers can be a blessing. Single mothers are able to go on the network and share ideas, suggestions, and simple life hacks about managing a household while working and raising children in a single parent home. Starting a blog or social media page will allow you to have someone to talk to when in need of just plain adult conversation, and the possibility of creating life-long friends. Hosting a virtual meeting will allow you to connect with other mothers from around the world who share the same interest in various topics about motherhood. Creating a network will set up a platform to uplift, inspire and encourage other single mothers, while you yourself are being encouraged, uplifted and inspired. So it's a win-win situation. There may be single mothers somewhere who absolutely have no one to carry on adult conversations with, and are suffering from "coupedup-mom syndrome". In other words, the mom is in the house with the kids *all* day. Being trapped in the house with children all day can be overwhelming and strenuous, and you may begin to crave adult conversation and interactions, to be able to vent to someone, and to receive emotional and social support. You may need adult contact so you can talk about ideas to other single moms on how to handle the day-to-day household chores while managing children, keeping order in your home, and trying to not going stir-crazy. There are some areas that have support groups for single moms that have face-to-face meetings. Child care services are provided while you socialize with other single moms. This provides a break from the children, and will allow you to be in the presence of other single moms to vent to, bounce ideas off of, get suggestions from, and to offer suggestions that can be of advantage to them.

Networking can be done anywhere: in the mall, grocery store, beauty salon, women's conferences, church, or other community locations. My church recently held a book signing platform for all the authors within our church. This gave me an opportunity to network with them. You see, they had already been where I was trying to go! So of course, I was able to pick their brains, and obtain valuable information that would help me to get where they were; which was to have my written work manifested and tangible in book form, also. I saw this as a divine opportunity for me, that God laid it on my pastor's heart to hold a book signing with authors in our church. However, this also gave me an opportunity to support and sow a seed into the authors in my local church, by buying their books. Motivated by the authors, I was believing for my own written work to be published.

I recently attended a women's conference that was being held within my area with a group of ladies consisting of cousins and mutual friends. I was able to connect with women who had similar things in common with me. Some of the women had already achieved and overcame things that I currently desired to achieve. Therefore, it was easier for me to ask questions and get their expertise and counsel on what I need to do and not do. I strongly believe that knowing what not to do is just as important as knowing what to do. This knowledge can save you time, and keep you from setting yourself back. At the time I attended the conference, I had two books that I was working on. One of which you are currently holding in your hand (To God Be The Glory-TGBTG). However, let me back up for a moment.

A couple weeks before the conference, I had heard God tell me to start looking for an editor and a publisher, as I was close to completing this book. I said, "*Okay, God.*" So, I began browsing the internet for editors and publishers in the area. I came across a website that had a list of editors and publishers in various areas. I researched their history in book editing and book publishing, I read reviews of their clients, and I looked into the categories they had the most experience in. There were some who had experience in essay writing using various formats for college students . Others specialized in business proposals, dissertations and resumes. I knew I did not want to go with an editor who only specified in writing resumes or dissertations; as that did not fit in with the required support needed for my book. Plus these companies were four hours or more from where I lived, and I prefer to be in driving distance in case I need to conduct business face-to-face. I browsed again, and saw one publishing company that was located a half-hour from where I lived, and had good reviews, and had experience working with authors who produced similar to the same style books that I was writing. Yet, for whatever reason, I did not look into it further. Perhaps, I got distracted by something else (by the way, distraction is of the enemy). Then, in my prayer time, I said, "Lord, order my steps, direct and guide me to a book editor/publisher that I'm supposed to be with, who will meet my needs." Fast forward two weeks. Now, I'm at the women's conference, and one of the speakers at the women's conference just so happened to be the owner of a book publishing company that was located within my area. The publishing company had experience working with authors with writing styles and book layouts similar to mine. And it just so happens, it was the same company that I had seen online during my search, but got distracted and didn't go further. I was extremely elated; I knew my steps were ordered and that God had set up divine connections for the owner of this particular publishing company to be at the same women's conference I was attending.

I was also able to actually meet with, and introduce myself to the owner of the publishing company. I learned that she also provided other services that were of interest to me for some other things that I want to work on in the future. I was also able to network with other business owners who were vendors at the women's conference. Each one of these entrepreneurs and business women handled their business like a BOSS! That all the more inspired me to dream BIG, and to see myself doing the things that God has laid on my heart to do, and to be and to do them fearlessly. I have learned that in order to get to where you want to go, it is important to surround yourself with people who are where you want to go, and have done the things that God has purposed in your heart to do.

A dear friend of mine, who is well-seasoned spiritually, and sharp as a tack intellectually, is still ambitious despite her age. In my eyes, she has hit the second prime of her life! My friend, who just finished her doctorate degree, and is also an author among other amazing things that she has accomplished, is a big inspiration to me. Not long ago, I was able to sit down with her and talk about some things, and just allow her to pour knowledge and wisdom into me; it was priceless! Ask God for divine connections and to send people into your life who you can network with, and who can pour into you and inspire you. Also, ask God to send those to you whom you can uplift and inspire. Someone is looking at you, Sis, and wanting to know how you got to where you are. Yes, even though you may not think you have it all together, to someone else, you are their example, and they want to get to where you are. So, ask God to show you, or send you someone who you can help to uplift, encourage and inspire. Then pour into them all that you have learned and experienced!

Scriptures:

The steps of a (good and righteous) man are directed and established by the Lord, And He delights in his way (and blesses his path).
Psalm 37:23 (AMP)

This Book of the Law shall not depart from your mouth, but you shall meditate on it day and night, that you may observe and do according to all that is written in it. For then you shall make you way prosperous, and then you shall deal wisely and have good success.
Joshua 1:8 (AMPC)

Where there is no (wise, intelligent) guidance, the people fall (and go off course like a ship without a helm), But in the abundance of (wise and Godly) counselors there is victory.
Proverbs 11:14 (AMP)

As iron sharpens iron, So a man sharpens (and influences) another (through discussion).
Proverbs 27:17 (AMP)

The Lord will open for you His good treasure house, the heavens, to give rain to your land in its season and to bless all the work of your hand.
Deuteronomy 28:12 (AMP)

Confession For God To Send Divine Destiny Helpers

Heavenly Father,

You are the King of Kings and the Lord of Lords, without You, I am nothing. Lord, I thank you for guiding my steps and giving divine connections to people who are of sound wisdom, knowledge, and understanding whom I can glean from. Thank you, Lord, for strategically placing the right people in my life who are already where you are taking me and who are already where you want me to go so that I can be inspired by and be challenged to grow higher and higher in all areas of my life, for placing those in my circle who can sharpen me and give wise counsel. Thank you, Lord, that you have promised in your word that as I mediate on your word, and observe and do according to it, that you will cause me to deal wisely and have good success.

Thank you for blessing the works of my hands.

In Jesus Name,

Amen

CHAPTER 18
He is Faithful to Us!

Being a single mom comes with ups, downs, good times, and bad times. However, through it all, I want you to know that God sees you, and He is concerned with every little detail that involves you and your children. We must learn to cast our cares upon Him, for He cares for us. (1Peter 5:7) Being a single mom is a great sacrifice, but it is a rewarding sacrifice. Although we may feel like the entire world is on our shoulders, it is important to remember not to dwell on the negatives, but to dwell on the positives and keep in mind that you are not alone. If we are not careful, we can allow the enemy to sap us of all of our joy, strength, happiness, faith and hope. The enemy will steal them right out from under us if we continually dwell on the negative.

In John 10:10, it says, *the thief only comes only to steal and kill and to destroy*. The enemy would like nothing more than to *sift us as wheat*, which is why it is so important that we get before God daily and pray and spend time with him; asking for His guidance and protection. We must spend time reading His word so that we can keep ourselves built up in faith and able to stand on His promises (His word). When we stay built up in God through prayer and reading and standing on His word, that is what keeps us from day to day. Writing down or journaling during your prayer time with God is important. Recording everything you hear the Spirit of the Lord say to you as you commune with Him during your prayer time, is so important. Keeping a record of what God says to you daily is important; especially during the storms of life when you need to be reminded on God's Love for you. My Pastor once said, "Don't doubt in the dark, what God spoke to you in the Light". Keep a journal of what you hear from God during your prayer time, or the certain scriptures that just "jump out at you" when you're reading your bible. The information is important; it is a way of God calling your attention toward a particular thing.

Keeping a prayer journal, and aside from that, keeping a notebook specifically for answered prayers, is also important. The book of answered prayers is for those times when you can't see your way, and you are struggling to trust God. The book of answered prayers is for that time when you're having a situation that has "popped off" in your life, and you don't know what to do. It is for that time when you have prayed to God about a situation and you haven't heard an answer yet. Those are the times to refer back to your notebook of answered prayers; it will help keep you grounded as you reflect back on how faithful God has been towards you in past circumstances. You will have a tangible record of God's faithfulness to you; His personal track record that He has established with you that you can reflect back on to keep you in faith. The book of prayers helps you know that you can expect God to come through for you with an answer to your prayers. 2 Timothy 2:13 says, *if we are faithless,*

He remains faithful, for he cannot disown himself. Hallelujah! God is a faithful God even when we are faithless.

Everything is constantly changing in the world and nothing is constant; things in the world are unsteady and rocky and it feels like nothing is the same from day to day. Yet, we can rest assured that our God is constant and He will never change. We can be sure that with God we can remain stable in unstable times; as it is written in Hebrews 13:8, *Jesus Christ is the same yesterday, today, and forever.* Malachi 3:6 says, *for I am the Lord, I change not; therefore, you sons of Jacob are not consumed.* God is our firm foundation, our solid rock on which we can stand, depend, on and trust in (Matthew 7: 24-27). He will not, and cannot fail us, or let us down! Amen.

So, as a single parent, sometimes we may find it a little difficult to trust God; especially when we are walking in uncharted waters. However, rest assured that He is faithful, He is a God who cannot lie. What He says he will do, He will do! We can take it to the bank! We are parents to children He entrusted us with. Likewise, Jesus is our parent, and He takes care of us, guides, leads, and provides for us. Therefore, we must be good stewards over what belongs to Him; our children belong to Him. We must be leading, guiding and protecting them; and raising them to be all that they were called to be in Christ. Knowing that we have a Higher Power that we as parents can depend on, just as we have little ones who depend on us is comforting. Not saying that every day will be perfect. But knowing that God is with us, and is on our side, we can rest assured that God being for us is more than the whole world against us! (Romans 8:31)

Scriptures on His Faithfulness

The Lord is faithful, who will establish you and guard you from the evil one.
2 Thessalonians 3:3 (NKJV)

Your faithfulness endures to all generations; you have established the earth, and it stands fast.
Psalms 119:90 (NKJV)

God is faithful, by whom you were called into the fellowship of his son, Jesus Christ our Lord.
1Corinthians 1:9 (NKJV)

Let us hold fast the confession of our faith without wavering, for he who promised is faithful.
Hebrews 10:23 (NKJV)

Confession Acknowledging God's Faithfulness

Heavenly Father,

When things seem unstable and are always changing, God, I thank you that I can come to you because you are so loyal and faithful. You are constant and you change not! I have peace knowing that I have stability in you. God, I thank you that I can lift mine eyes and look to the hills, to where my help comes from. (Psalm 121) Lord, when I want to worry, help me to remember to cast my cares on you, because you care for me. (1Peter 5:7) Lord, I thank you that you have worked all things out for my good (Romans 8:28). I thank you for being true to your word and backing up your promises. Your word will not return void nor will it fall to the ground and it will accomplish all to which you set out for it to do (Isaiah 55:11). God, I thank you that you remain faithful even when I have moments when I am faithless. God I am forever grateful that I have been called into fellowship with your son Jesus.

In Jesus Name,
Amen

CHAPTER 19
God Will Restore

Often times bad break ups, or a divorce, can leave our hearts in shambles. We can become bitter in heart, feel betrayed, broken, or wounded. Sometimes when we think we have moved on, and have gotten past whatever the situation or circumstance may have been, without even realizing it we can still be holding unforgiveness in our hearts. You may ask, "How can I detect whether or not I have forgiven a person?" A key sign is when you hear the person's name and you feel something rising up on the inside of you that is similar to anger or rage. That is a sign that you have not forgiven the person. If when you hear that the person who wronged you is doing well and is successful, and you feel resentment, or you think to yourself, "Why are they so happy when they did such and such to me... then you have unforgiveness in your heart toward that person. When we don't deal with a hurt or an offense, any unforgiveness in our heart left "unchecked", can take root and turn into bitterness.

The bible says that the "root of bitterness" springs up and causes trouble, and by it, <u>many</u> become defiled (Hebrews 12:15). Bitterness defiles us before the Lord, and causes no end of trouble in our own lives and *in the lives of others, too*. I look at bitterness and unforgiveness as an open wound of the heart. For instance, for a while, I was upset with the father of my child because I wanted him to be more involved with our child than he was. Despite the fact that we are not together, I still want him to be a father to his son. So for a while I went around with unforgiveness in my heart because I'm thinking to myself, "How can a parent who lives in the same city as their child, only communicate and physically see their child a handful of times in a year?? I mean who does that??" At that time, I was operating in unforgiveness because, here I am, I see such potential and an awesomeness our son possesses, that even <u>strangers</u> come up to us, and say they see greatness in him. Like, what father do you know who would not want to be a part of his son's life, whom others can see is so full of greatness?? But I began to realize that I had to forgive, not for my son's father, but for me, and also for my son. I did not want to bleed onto my son, from my open wound of unforgiveness and bitterness. When we allow wounds to remain open, as long as they are open, they bleed. The bible verse says that <u>many</u> are defiled from bitterness. So, who closest to us are we going to bleed on…Our children!!

Bleeding onto our children looks like:

1.) Talking bad about the non-custodial parent in front of our children.
2.) Telling our children they will be like their no-good daddy or momma.
3.) Keeping our children away from the non-custodial parent (there are non-custodial who parents do wish to see their kids but the custodial parent keeps them away on purpose.
4.) Keeping the non-custodial parent from having any contact or communication with their child or any of the child's family on the non-custodial parent's side.

    It is so important that we take time to allow God to heal our wounds, and make us whole so that we can forgive,. so that we don't bleed onto our children. I have had this discussion with some of my family and friends who are single parents. We often say, don't talk bad about the other parent. If the child asks about the absent parent(who is not there because we know they don't want to have anything to do with the child) we don't talk bad about the other parent to the child. We know that eventually, as that child gets older, that child will come to their own conclusion, and make their own judgement about the absent parent, without the single mom having to say anything negative to your child about the absent parent.

The beauty of all this is that God sees all, he hears all and He knows! So in saying that God will restore to you what the cankerworm and locusts have eaten. God is not going to just let you be depleted and not restore you back to health and wholeness (in heart and mind) No, He will restore and give you back double for your trouble! Yes, I am a witness, I have seen it in my son's life. No, my son's dad is not in his life like I would like for him to be. HOWEVER, GOD has placed Godly Men in his life that take up the slack of what he is not getting from having that consistent father figure in his life. Divine connections have been made in every aspect of my son's life, in various environments. These connections have been made at school, at church, at the barbershop where he gets his haircuts, and with his coaches in each sport he plays. I can pin-point at least one and in some cases two or more male role models in each setting, that God has divinely placed in my son's path who have poured into him. They take up time with him so that he can see what it is to be a man; a godly man, a man of integrity, a man who worships and praises God, a man who is hardworking, a man who is faithful, and a man who knows what it requires to be a family man! And for that I am so grateful.

To my single parents who are raising young men, and you have no consistent, positive male influences around, your job is to cover your sons in prayer. Pray that God will send divine connections; godly, male role models for your sons, to help guide them and direct them and to pour into them! Hallelujah!! God will do it! Yes, He will! I am a living witness because He has done so for my son. Yes, for that I am forever grateful. There was a time when my son was younger, I said to myself, "How am I going to raise him to be a man? To show him how to take responsibility like a man should?" But God! He will make a way and put the right male presence in place at the right time to pour spiritual insight, wisdom, and knowledge into your sons.

Not only is God a way-maker, but He is also a restorer. Have you been run down, depleted of all your energy and emotions, or felt like you couldn't give of yourself to your children like you should? Good news, God can restore you, Sis! He can restore back to your life, the vitality, health, peace of mind or whatever it is that has been depleted in your life. God can restore back to you what the enemy has stolen from you! His will is for you to receive double for your trouble! God can restore you mentally, physically, emotionally and psychologically. He can and will heal your hurts and your wounds, He will make you whole. But you've got to forgive; drop and let go of holding onto the hurt and offenses that causes bitterness, and resentment, and hardens our hearts toward man and toward God. Allow God to soften and heal your heart, and watch God pick up the shambles of your heart, and mend you, and put you back together again, in front of the very ones who broke you. Just ask God to heal you and to perfect that which concerns you. Sometimes we may try to get even and avenge the wrongs that have done to us. But we must learn to allow God to fight our battles (Exodus 14:14). God says, *who will dare to contend with Me?* (Isaiah50:8 AMP) God says, recompense, I will repay (Rom 12:19). Jesus is your vindicator

(Psalm7:6). He says, Touch not my anointed and do my prophets no harm (Psalm 105: 15). Know that God has your back! God sees you, Sis; His hand is on you and your children. Trust Him and you will not go wrong; He has you and your children in the palm of His hands. Allow God to heal you in whatever way that looks like for you, because the process of healing does not look the same for everybody. Allow God to deal with your heart, ask God to show you who to forgive so that you can forgive those who have hurt you, so that you can begin the healing process. And yes, sometimes it takes more than one time to forgive someone; especially when you've been holding to the hurt and offense for a long time. Just decide to continue to forgive them until you can say that person's name, and not feel any animosity towards them. Forgiveness is for you; not for them, so you can be free! Like my pastor says, "It's like getting them off your hook, and putting them on God's hook." Let God deal with them. He can do a far better job dealing with those who have hurt or offended us than we ourselves can. Even Jesus asked God the Father to forgive those who did Him wrong. When Jesus was hanging on the cross, in Luke 23:34 He said, "Father forgive them, for they know not what they are doing", as the soldiers divided up His clothes by casting lots 23(Luke 23:34). So forgive. Be free. Live free!

Scriptures

And when you stand praying, if you hold anything against anyone, forgive them, so that your Father in heaven may forgive your sins.
Mark 11:25 (NIV)

Because you got a double dose of trouble and more than your share of contempt, your inheritance in the land will be doubled and your joy go on forever.
Isaiah 61:7 (MSG)

For I will restore you to health and heal your wounds declares the Lord.
Jeremiah 30:17a (NIV)

I will restore to you the years that the locust and canker worm hath eaten.
Joel 2:25 (NIV)

He heals the brokenhearted and binds up their wounds.
Psalm 147:3 (NIV)

Confessions for Restoration and Release of Unforgiveness and Bitterness and Healing of the Heart from Past Hurts

Lord,

I come to you and ask that you show me my heart. Lord, anything that I am holding on to, Lord that is keeping me tied to my past and keeping me from moving forward into the very best that you have for me. I ask that you reveal it to me so that I can let go and release the person(s) so that my heart will be set free from unforgiveness and bitterness and resentment. Lord, If I am holding any unforgiveness, resentment or bitterness, against the absent parent, I choose to forgive them, Lord.

Lord, help me to let go of the offense and the hurt so that I can move forward and allow you to begin to heal me. Heal me Lord, so that I will no longer bleed onto my child(ren) my negative thoughts, and opinions of the absent parent. Lord help me, as I cannot do this alone. God, if I find myself holding onto it again, help me to remember to drop it again, and let it go, and to keep a forgiving heart. Thank you, Lord, for healing my broken heart and binding my wounds. I thank you for restoring back to me all that has been lost. I thank you that you are near to me, for your word says that you are close to them who are of broken heart and of a contrite spirit. Thank you, Lord, that my heart is healed and whole, and for restoring me so that I can move forward in the best of blessings that you have for me.

In Jesus Name,

Amen

Confession Over Our Sons

Heavenly Father,

I thank you for entrusting me with my son(s). I thank you that you are a father to the fatherless. Give me the grace, strength and wisdom I need to raise a champion for Jesus! Lord, I pray for divine connections for my son(s), that you place godly, male role models in their paths. Godly, male role models that are willing to pour into my son(s), and are an example to them of what it is like to be a man after God's own heart. I thank you Lord, that you will compensate for what was missing and broken in his life. Thank you for doing that for my son(s), God, so that they can see godly men of integrity who follow after you and in the things of you, God. I thank you that my son(s) has a teachable spirit, and is a young man of integrity. Father, I thank you that my son(s) sees himself the way you see him. I thank you that my son(s) is confident in Christ, bold, courageous, smart, intelligent and witty. I am grateful that he has a healthy self-esteem and a healthy self-image about himself. Father, I thank you that my son(s) is a leader and not a follower, the head and not the tail, above only and never beneath. I speak the favor of God over his life! I decree and declare that he will not be a victim of police brutality or any heinous acts or crimes because of fear of society and injustices in the world because he is covered in the Blood of Jesus. I decree and declare long life over his life, my son will see many days if Jesus tarries. I decree and declare the precious Blood of Jesus over my son(s) in Jesus Name, he will be and do all that you have purposed for him to be and do in this earth. I speak life over him, I speak health in his mind and body, I decree and declare that favor surrounds him as a shield. I thank you that he has favor with God and man, his teachers and peers. God, I thank you for going before him and keeping him in his coming out and going in. I decree and declare that angels are surrounding him and keeping his feet from stumbling, God. I decree and declare that everything my son(s) put his hands to do is blessed. I cancel the plans of the enemy over his life, in Jesus Name. I thank you that my son(s) is a Winner! I decree and declare my son is wise beyond his years.

In Jesus Name, Amen

Confession Over Our Daughters

Heavenly Father,

I thank you for entrusting me with a beautiful daughter(s). I pray that you give me grace to set an example before her. Give me grace, wisdom and strength to raise her to be a mighty woman of God. Lord, I pray that my daughter is a leader in her generation, my daughter(s) is a leader and not a follower, she is the head and not the tail, she is above only and not beneath. Lord, I thank you that my daughter possesses a healthy self-esteem and healthy self-image of herself. I thank you that she is confident, bold, smart, intelligent, courageous and that she grows to have a heart for God and the things of God. Thank you, Father God, that she will see herself the way you see her. Help me Lord, to carry myself in a way that glorifies you, Lord, so that my daughter(s) will see how to carry herself always in a manner that glorifies you. I thank you that favor surrounds my daughter as a shield, I thank you that everything she puts her hands to do is blessed. She is blessed going in and coming out.

I thank you Lord, that she has favor with God and man, her teachers and her peers. I decree and declare that she will not be a victim of police brutality or any heinous acts or crimes because of fear of society and injustices in the world, because she is covered in the Blood of Jesus. I decree and declare long life over her. I speak life over her and I speak health to her mind and body. I plead the blood of Jesus over my daughter. Thank you God for keeping her in all her ways. Thank you Lord, that she will be and do all that you have created her to be and do in the earth in Jesus Name. I decree and declare she is God's earthen vessel, created for God's use and purpose in the earth. She will fulfil her God-given assignment and call here in the earth. I cancel the plans of the enemy over her life right now in Jesus Name! I decree and declare my daughter is a Winner! Lord, I give you all the praise, thanks and glory for it!

In Jesus Name, Amen

CHAPTER 20
The Favor of God

The psalmist said, *Oh, taste and see that the LORD (our God) is good; How blessed [fortunate, prosperous, and favored by God] is the man who takes refuge in Him.* (Psalm 34:8) As I look back from the time my son was born to now, I am in awe of how God truly demonstrated, and continues to demonstrate His favor in the lives of my son and I. I can say that when things looked dim and I could not see a way through, God always made a way! That tells me that His promise to me that He will *not withhold no good thing from me* is truth! His word is truth without error! My son has been attending private school since he was in the third grade, and I cannot count not one time when I was unable to pay the tuition fee, daycare fee, or lunch fee. Now, sometimes the daycare fees and lunch fees may have gotten behind; and yes, there were times I received reminder letters from the school about past due monies on lunch accounts and day care accounts because my money was being stretched. However, God has always provided a way!

I am reminded of the story in the bible when Abraham obeyed God and went to sacrifice his only son, Isaac to God. Somebody say, "BUT GOD!!" God had a ram in the bush for Abraham to sacrifice instead of His son! (Genesis 22: 1-13). Let me tell you, God will provide you a ram in the bush when it seems like there is no other way. I've never had to borrow money; nor have I had to take out a loan to pay for school-related fees for my son to participate in extracurricular activities like band and sports. To God be the Glory! I'm reminded when my son wanted to play the trombone and joined the band. A trombone is not too expensive, but it definitely is not cheap either, when you consider my budget at that time. So, God hooked up a divine connection, and I was able to get a brand-new trombone within my budget, in comparison to the cost of other trombones. It was also a good brand, known for high quality. And I'm not saying all of this to brag or to boast. But I am truly grateful for God's grace and favor on us; which has allowed me, as a single mother, to be able to financially handle tuitions and other bills on a single income. I have been able to handle financial obligations that some families can't with two incomes coming in.

I heard someone say that "one day of favor is worth a lifetime of labor". That is so true, God's favor on your life can take you farther than you could ever go on your own. The favor of God can cause an employer to choose your application out of one hundred applications. When your ways please the Lord, God draws His favor on you; the bible says that even your enemies will be at peace with you (Proverbs 16:7 EXB). The favor of God can cause your name to rise from the bottom of the waiting list to the top of the waiting list. The grace and favor of God will give you the strength you need to do all that He has called you to do! Furthermore, I am reminded that God is not a *respecter of person*. (Romans 2:11 AMP) What He does in principle for one, He has to do in principle for another. So, let me encourage you. With God on your side, you and God are a majority! Whatever situation you may face, remember God is in you, He is with, and He is for you! The grace and the favor of God is on you, to see you through, and to bring you into His best for you. God is always looking out for us. He knows where we are in life, and His eyes are constantly on us, even in the intricate details of our life. He sees and He is aware. Ask God to shower you with His favor in every area of your life, then acknowledge Him for His actions, and give Him all the thanks and the praise, because he deserves it.

Scriptures

And may the Lord our God favor us and give us success. May he give permanence to all we do.
Psalm 90:17 (TLB)

For the Lord God is a sun and shield; The Lord bestows grace and favor and honor; No good thing will He withhold from those who walk uprightly.
Psalm 84:11 (AMP)

So find favor and high esteem in the sight of God and man.
Proverbs 3:4 (AMP)

For You, O Lord, bless the righteous man (the one who is in right standing with You); you surround him with favor as with a shield.
Psalm 5:12 (AMP)

Confession For The Favor of God

Heavenly Father,

I thank you for your favor that surrounds me as a shield and that I find favor in the sight of God and man. Lord, I trust you and I thank you that no good thing will you withhold from me, and I thank you that you look favorably upon me just like you did with Elizabeth and Mary in the bible (Luke 1:24-25;28-30 AMP) because you are no respecter of persons. I believe that the favor of God is in my life, and at work in my life, and my children's lives. Everywhere we go, we see the favor of God on our lives, and Lord, I thank you for it.

In Jesus Name,
Amen

Single Mom
NUGGET NOTES

CHAPTER 21
Be Encouraged!

Dear single mom (you), let me encourage you. You may feel unappreciated undervalued and unworthy. You may feel like you have no life, and all that you are, is wrapped up in the responsibilities of being a mom. Sometimes, you may feel bogged down or overwhelmed; but let me encourage you! It gets better! Things change and seasons change. What you may find yourself dealing with today, will work itself out if you keep going. Keep doing good. Keep doing right by your children. Keep loving them through every period of their life and through every stage they may be in. As I look back over the years, from where my son and I used to be to where we are now, I realize not only have my son and I gone through some season difficulties, we have also GROWN through some seasons of difficulties together. There have been times when it was like, "Either, it's gone to be me, or you!" I'm sure some of you have heard your mama say, "I brought you into this world and I will take you out"! There may be some seasons when you and your child may experience difficulties. Let me encourage you to not just go through it, but to grow through it. One day your child will see all the sacrifices you have made, and as they grow and understand, they will come to know and appreciate all that you do for them. When your teenager walks up to you, and throws their arms around you, and says, "Thank you mom for all you do, I love you", your heart will smile. When you find out through your child's teacher that your child writes an essay on *who is your greatest role model,* and it's all about you, your heart will smile. When you see the love displayed through your child's Mother's Day card, with its hand-drawn stick figure picture of you from your five-year-old, your heart will smile. I believe that there is a special grace and strength that God gives to us single mothers. I pray God continues to give us grace and strength to raise healthy and smart children who are first class citizens, and first-class leaders who are world changers and world overcomers! Being a single mom comes with great sacrifices, however; we reap great rewards!!

Scriptures for Encouragement:

And let us not grow weary in well doing; for in due season we shall reap, if we faint not.
Galatians 6:9 (KJV)

"Had it not been for the Lord who was on my side, Let Israel now say".
Psalm 124:1 (KJV)

I will lift mine eyes unto the hills from whence cometh my help.
Psalm 121:1 (KJV)

Fear not, for I am your God. I will strengthen you, Yes, I will help you, I will uphold you with My righteous right hand.
Isaiah 41:10 (NKJV)

Peace I leave with you; my peace I give you. I do not give to you as the world gives. Do not let your hearts be troubled and do not be afraid.
John14:27 (NKJV)

Confession for Encouragement

Heavenly Father,

I thank you that through your word I am encouraged. Thank you for giving me the strength and grace I need to be a good steward over the children you have entrusted me with. Thank you Lord that as I wait upon you, you are renewing my strength so that I will not grow weary in well-doing so that I may reap a harvest. I thank you for putting your supernatural on my natural to get the job done, for I can do all things through Christ whom strengthens me, and with you all things have been made possible, for nothing is impossible with you. Thank you for energizing my body and my mind, as I operate in my role as a mother. I thank you for giving me patience and understanding. Help me Lord, to remember to lean not to my understanding but in all my ways to acknowledge you to direct my path. Thank you that I can look to the hills for where my help comes, because if it weren't for you on my side Lord, I don't know where I would be. But thank you Lord that you see fit to continue to keep me, sustain and guide me through each and every situation and circumstance.

Lord, I thank you that your eyes are on me, and you see me and where I am in this walk with you, thank you for upholding me with your righteous right hand and keeping my feet from falling. I thank you for your hand that is on my life and my children's lives. Lord, help me to totally depend on you in every area of my life, knowing that you will never leave me nor forsake me. Thank you, Lord, that I am secure in you because of your love for me. I thank you that Your Love will never fail. So, Lord, I thank you for your grace and your mercy. I thank you for exchanging my weakness for your strength.

In Jesus Name,
Amen

Salvation Prayer

Say this prayer out loud:

Heavenly Father,

I believe that Jesus died on the cross for my sins. I believe in my heart that God raised Jesus from the dead. I invite you Jesus to come into my heart and I make you my Lord and Savior. I confess you as the Lord of my life, thank you Father for sending your son, Jesus to save me.

In Jesus Name,
Amen

Romans 10:9-10 KJV

If you said this prayer, you are now SAVED! WELCOME! WELCOME TO THE FAMILY OF GOD! I encourage you to ask God to guide you to a good, bible teaching church where you can continue to grow in the Lord.

~Shalom

Single Mom
the Great yet Rewarding Sacrifice

Speak Life

AUTHOR CHARITY RICKS

AUTHOR CHARITY RICKS

Author Charity Ricks is an entrepreneur, independent retailer, and CEO of Allpoint Scrubs International. She was born in Rocky Mount, North Carolina and grew up in Nashville, North Carolina. Charity is a proud mother of one son. She holds an Associate Degree in Applied Health Sciences and works as a Physical Therapist Assistant.

Becoming a single mother at an early age, Author Charity Ricks felt led by inspiration to encourage, uplift, and inspire other single moms by sharing how she uses her faith to overcome past and present parenting challenges. Through each chapter, she shares faith-based confessions to encourage the reader to speak life, giving words over themselves and their child(ren). She hopes that this book will reach single moms around the world to serve as a faith-based resource guide while highlighting her **Great yet Rewarding Sacrifice**.

Connect with Author Charity Ricks at:
charityricks1@gmail.com

shero publishing

Made in the USA
Middletown, DE
25 February 2023

25291967R00089